First
Certificate
GOLD
Practice Exams

WITH KEY

Amos Paran

Addison Wesley Longman Limited
Edinburgh Gate, Harlow,
Essex, CM20 2JE England
and Associated Companies throughout the world.

First published 1996

Fourth impression 1997

Set in Adobe Frutiger 55 Roman 11/14pt

Printed in Spain by Gráficas Estella

ISBN 0582 27920 8

Author's acknowledgements
I would like to thank Richard Acklam, Sally Burgess and
Christine Lindop for their helpful comments on the manu-
script; Judith King for her support; and Frances Woodward
for her comments and unwavering good humour and
patience throughout the editorial process.

We are grateful to the following for permission to reproduce
copyright material:

The Big Issue for an extract from the article 'Is there a
woman in the house' by Sharon Garfinkle in *The Big Issue*,
issue 117, February 1995; A & C Black (Publishing) Ltd for an
extract from *Cruising with children* by Gwenda Cornell, published Adlard Coles 1986; BBC Worldwide Publishing for a
slightly adapted extract based on the article '*My Kind* of Day'
by Nick Smurthwaite in *Radio Times*, 19.5.1990; Cyclists'
Touring Club for an adapted extract from the article 'Women
and Cycling' by Pat Strauss in *Cycling, Touring and
Campaigning Magazine*, June/July 1995; Ewan Macnaughton
Associates for adapted extracts from the articles 'Planners
sound the alarm over man burgled 16 times' by A. J McIlroy
in *Daily Telegraph*, 13.8.91 & 'Rogue twins who left their
dabs on crime detection' by David Millward in *Daily
Telegraph* 3.9.91; Dominion Press for adaptations based on
the articles 'School Leaver Interview' – Jilly Halliday, 'Sky TV
Presenter' & 'Working Adventures Abroad' by Sarah Eykyn in
School Leaver Magazine, vol. 25 No.4; Express Newspapers
plc for an adapted extract based on the article 'Danger when
a computer becomes your best friend' by Melanie
Whitehouse in *Daily Express*, 15.1.90; the author, William
Green for adapted extracts from his article 'Take flight in a
soaring kite' in *The Sunday Times* 12.11.89 © William
Green/The Times, 1989; Guardian News Services for adapted
extracts from the articles 'Double trouble looms for two of a
kind' by John Illman in *The Guardian*, 22.6.90, 'The home-
made television made from scrap' in *The Guardian* 12.2.91,
'... about Traffic Lights'. by Andrew McLachlan in *The
Guardian* 25.2.91 & 'Not enough fish in the sea' in *Education
Guardian* 11.4.94; Haynes Publishing for an adaptation of the
introduction to *Action Sports* by Nick Crane, published by

Oxford Illustrated Press, Sparkford, Nr. Yeovil, Somerset,
BA22 7JJ.

Sample OMR answer sheets are reproduced by permission of
the University of Cambridge Local Examinations Syndicate.

We are grateful to the following for permission to reproduce
copyright photographs:

Ace Photo library/Marka for 124t/Roger Howard for 121b,
Addison Wesley Longman Ltd/Gareth Boden for 56r,56b,56t,
The Image Bank for 118t/D Redfearn for 98/Terry Williams for
126t, Pictor International for 115b,115t, Robert Harding
Picture Library for 123b,126b, Telegraph Colour Library for
118b,119bl,119br,119ml,119tl,119tm,119tr,120t,
120b,121t, Tony Stone Images/Chad Slattery for 119cl/Ed
Honowitz for 123t/Jon Bradley for 117b/Mark Segal for
117b/Peter Correz for 124b, Elizabeth Whiting Associates for
114b,114t,127t,127b.

Designed by Linda Males

Illustrated by Caroline Logan

Contents

Introduction

First Certificate Gold Practice Exams is a collection of five practice exams designed to meet the needs of candidates preparing for the Revised First Certificate Examination. It accompanies the *First Certificate Gold Coursebook* and the *First Certificate Gold Exam Maximiser*, but the material is not course-linked and can therefore be used independently of any coursebook. It covers all five papers and has been written to suit the guidelines published in the Specifications for the Revised FCE Examination. The book is accompanied by two cassettes which include the material for Paper 4 – Listening. The *With Key* edition includes Answer Keys to all papers and the tapescripts of the cassettes.

Although the practice exams in this book are of approximately the same level of difficulty, the later exams are slightly more difficult than the earlier ones. For this reason it is advisable to do the exams in order. It is also best to start practising well in advance of the exam – this way candidates will have more time to see which areas need attention to.

Sample answer sheets

In Paper 1 (Reading), Paper 3 (Use of English) and Paper 4 (Listening) candidates mark or write their answers on special answer sheets. Examples of such answer sheets are provided on pages 109–112. It is permissible to photocopy the sample answer sheets so that candidates can have practice in writing their answers for each of the practice exams.

Exam information

Paper	Name	Timing	Content	Test focus
Paper 1	Reading	1 hour 15 minutes	4 long texts, or 3 long and 2 or more short texts; 35 reading comprehension questions.	Questions test candidates' understanding of the general idea, the main points, specific details, the structure of the text and specific information.
Paper 2	Writing	1 hour 30 minutes	Part 1: compulsory letter Part 2: a choice of writing tasks.	Questions test candidates' ability to write letters, reports, articles and compositions for specific audiences.
Paper 3	Use of English	1 hour 15 minutes	5 sections with 65 questions altogether focusing on grammar and vocabulary.	Questions test candidates' knowledge of grammar and vocabulary.
Paper 4	Listening	40 minutes (approximately)	2 longer recorded texts and 2 series of short extracts; 30 listening comprehension questions.	Questions test candidates' ability to understand the main idea, the main points, detail or specific information.
Paper 5	Speaking	15 minutes (approximately)	A conversation divided into four parts between two candidates and an interlocutor. Another examiner will be in the room to assess performance.	The four parts test candidates' ability to exchange personal and factual information, to express opinions and attitudes and to find out about other people's opinions and attitudes.

Practice exam 1

Paper 1 – Reading

PART 1

You are going to read parts of a leaflet about the Youth Hostels Association (YHA). Choose the most suitable heading from the list **A–I** for each part (**1–7**) of the leaflet. There is one extra heading which you do not need to use. There is an example at the beginning (**0**).
Mark your answers **on the separate answer sheet**.

A	Group facilities.
B	How do we keep the prices so low?
C	Group prices.
D	Local groups.
E	The countryside matters.
F	Travel the world!
G	What about the accommodation?
H	What does the price include?
I	How to book.

Youth Hostels Association

0	I

To avoid disappointment, especially during the summer months, it is best to enquire and make sure in advance that a bed is reserved for you. Just telephone the Hostel (before 1000 or after 1700 hours). At most Youth Hostels you can now pay by Visa and Access credit cards.

1	

What you pay to stay with us entitles you to use Hostel facilities such as showers and washrooms, drying rooms, lounge, self-catering kitchen and dining areas.

2	

Sleeping is in comfortable rooms which vary in size – from 4–6 beds to larger dormitories with around 8–16 beds. Blankets and pillows are included in the price for your overnight stay. You will need to either hire or buy a YHA sheet sleeping bag or you can bring your own sheets and pillow case.

3	

When staying at a Youth Hostel, we do ask you to help with some of the clearing up; usually something routine such as sweeping a floor or helping wash up. You also need to remember that Youth Hostels close for a period during the day – usually between 1000 and 1700 hours – and close for the night at 2300 hours. This helps to keep our running costs down.

4	

YHA is one of the leading environmental groups in Britain, helping to conserve Britain's unique landscape features and wildlife.

Members with an interest in conservation have the chance to carry out practical work – clearing out ponds, opening up footpaths and planting trees. So if you'd like to put something back into the landscape, now's your chance!

5	

We specialise in budget residential facilities for groups of young people. 28 of our Hostels offer field facilities and many have classrooms. *Datapack* is a publication designed for group leaders and contains details of those Youth Hostels which are particularly suitable for groups.

6	

If you like meeting people with similar interests and getting out and about in the countryside, then why not join a YHA group in your area? YHA groups organise regular social events and weekend activities – from discos and barbecues to theatre trips and country walks. Details of your nearest group can be found in the YHA Accommodation Guide.

7	

YHA is a member of the International Youth Hostel Federation and this means that once a member in England and Wales, you can stay at any Hostel showing the YHF sign. So whether you choose Europe or Australia, India or Peru, you can still stay with YHA. All you need to do is attach a recent photograph to your membership card and it becomes valid worldwide. And for recognised groups it's even simpler: International Leader cards enable groups of non-members – aged between 10 and 20 years – to stay in Youth Hostels, as long as they are accompanied by a YHA member who is aged 18 years or over!

PART 2

You are going to read an introduction to a book about action sports. For questions **8–14**, choose the answer (**A**, **B**, **C** or **D**) which you think fits best according to the text.
Mark your answers **on the separate answer sheet**.

Action Sports and Risk-Taking

Risk-takers have been taking part in action sports since the beginnings of time: the new challenge has always appealed to adventurous minds. The trick with risks is to understand the
5 possible dangers and then remove them by treating each as a problem with only one solution: the safe one. From the outside the game still looks 'risky', but to the risk-taker who understands the difficulties, the game is
10 a personal test of skill, rather than nerve. None of these sports *ought* to be dangerous; if they are, you're doing something wrong.

Risk-taking has other benefits. The best cure for a stressful working life may not be a week
15 flat-out on a beach; emptying the mind merely leaves it open for occupation by the home stresses which you brought with you. Pick up a new challenge, something that is exciting, stretching, new, and you not only
20 escape entirely from that other life, but return to it on a wave of confidence and strength that carries you over the problems which once seemed part of everyday life.

Action sports offer an escape, one where you
25 learn very quickly: in one week – or even in one weekend – you can learn more about yourself than you did all year. All inner fears disappear in the burn of concentration demanded by learning to fly, dive, ride or
30 climb. The pride earned through jumping from an aeroplane at 12,000 feet, or learning to roll a canoe, will stay with you for life. Then there are the other spin-offs: the mental

calm which comes with rock-climbing; the
35 wonderful colours of caves; the moment of freedom felt during that first flight beneath the wing of a glider. All these sports cause a wonderful thrill – be it dashing waves or free-falling through the air at 120 miles per hour –
40 but thrills are just a part of the story. Many of these sports double as types of travel. Horses, bicycles, skis, hot-air balloons can be used as vehicles for truly exotic journeys; journeys on which you can look at landscapes (and
45 yourself) from a new angle. And all of these are 'soft' vehicles; ones which allow you to move through, and feel for, the countryside, the mountains and deserts.

The sports in this book cover the complete
50 range of physical and mental skills: they can be done from your own doorstep or from any one of hundreds of places abroad. The sports demand from as little as the cost of a pair of boots to as much as it costs to buy a flying
55 machine. Some of them are very easily reached (I have a friend who goes gliding in his lunch-break), while others require travelling-time and complex equipment.

Finally, remember that each action sport is a
60 wonderful experience, and the more experiences we have, the richer we become, and the more we have to share.

Nick Crane

8 According to the writer, action sports

- **A** show a person's ability to overcome difficulties.
- **B** are dangerous because of the risks they involve.
- **C** test the daring of the person who does them.
- **D** are far more interesting than playing games.

9 The word 'it' in line 21 refers to

- **A** any holiday activity.
- **B** life at home and at work.
- **C** any action sport.
- **D** a challenging new activity.

10 What is the best type of holiday according to the writer?

- **A** Lying on the beach and doing nothing.
- **B** Engaging in something you are confident about.
- **C** Doing something you have never done before.
- **D** Escaping to a place which is totally new.

11 According to the writer, learning action sports

- **A** can be extremely frightening.
- **B** helps you learn to concentrate.
- **C** makes you understand yourself better.
- **D** is not really a difficult task at all.

12 Which of these advantages of action sports is **not** mentioned by the writer?

- **A** Maintaining fitness.
- **B** Experiencing thrills.
- **C** Building confidence.
- **D** Seeing new places.

13 'spin-offs' (line 33) are

- **A** action sports.
- **B** benefits.
- **C** achievements.
- **D** skills.

14 In general, the writer says that action sports

- **A** are inexpensive.
- **B** require a lot of time.
- **C** are extremely varied.
- **D** should not be done alone.

PART 3

You are going to read a newspaper article about a burglar alarm. Seven sentences have been removed from the article. Choose from the sentences **A–H** the one which fits each gap (**15–20**). There is one extra sentence which you do not need to use. There is an example at the beginning (**0**).
Mark your answers **on the separate answer sheet**.

PLANNERS SOUND THE ALARM OVER MAN BURGLED 16 TIMES

A former mayor of Hove in Sussex, who has been burgled 16 times in 18 years, has been ordered to remove the burglar alarm outside his 19th-century home. **0** **H**

'I got so fed up with being burgled that I had the alarm installed two and a half years ago,' said Mr Moy-Loader, 70, a former planning committee chairman. ' **15** But since the red box went up outside we haven't had a break-in and it is very comforting to know that it is there.'

Accusing the council of putting the appearance of property ahead of concern for the security of the people who live inside, he said: 'The object of having the box is so that it can be seen.'

' **16** They know I'm an expert on burglars' methods. After all, I've experienced 16 burglaries, including one in 1977 when I was badly beaten.'

17 'If for any reason we see anyone acting suspiciously, we can set off the alarm bell by pressing one of the buttons set at different parts of the house,' he said. While many people used mock burglar alarm boxes as a cheaper means of frightening off burglars, he said he preferred the comfort of knowing the box on his wall was the real thing.

Mr Roger Dowty, Hove council's conservation officer, said: 'Mr Moy-Loader appealed to the Department of the Environment when we insisted the bright red box should be moved. **18** '

'Our formal letter orders Mr Moy-Loader to take down the box, but we have made it clear that we are quite prepared to compromise if he moves it to a less noticeable place and paints it cream, the same colour as the buildings. Of course this means the box would not be seen from 50 yards or so away. **19** '

Mr Moy-Loader said last night that he had not been told by the council about a possible compromise if he repainted his alarm. ' **20** I cannot afford to take the issue to appeal in the High Court,' he said.

A But their inspector agreed with us that it was too obviously displayed.

B I am afraid I have no choice and it will have to come down.

C The Department of Environment's ruling in favour of the council meant that 10 other people in Hove conservation areas would now be served notice to move burglar alarm boxes that are too prominent.

D Mr Moy-Loader said his alarm gave him extra security because it was also connected to two alarm buttons in his home.

E The Police agree with me that it is an effective deterrent against the amateur burglar.

F We used to come back from holidays and find our home in a mess.

G Yet it would still be obvious to anyone about to try to break in.

H Council planners have told Mr Ian Moy-Loader, Conservative mayor in 1984–85, that the bright red box spoils the appearance of a row of houses in Brunswick Place, a conservation area.

PART 4

You are going to read excerpts from interviews with five students at the University of Luton. For questions **21–34** choose from the list of people (**A–E**). Some of the people may be chosen more than once. When more than one answer is required, these may be given in any order. There is an example at the beginning (**0**).
For question **35** choose the answer (**A**, **B**, **C**, or **D**) which you think fits best according to the text.
Mark your answers **on the separate answer sheet**.

Which of the interviewees:

had heard good opinions of the course before starting it?	**0** B	
were unemployed before starting the course?	**21**	**22**
enjoy mixing with people?	**23**	**24**
likes this university because of its geographical location?	**25**	
gives their story as an example to others?	**26**	
enjoys sports?	**27**	
is studying a subject unusual for their sex?	**28**	
has already made career progress as a result of their studies?	**29**	
feels that the course has changed their whole life?	**30**	
feels they are learning during leisure time as well?	**31**	
were supported by family members?	**32**	**33**
was worried about succeeding at university?	**34**	

35 What is the purpose of these interviews?

    A   To show the importance of higher education.
    B   To attract people from abroad to study in Britain.
    C   To attract students to the university.
    D   To show students some unusual career choices.

Emiko Asada	A

I'd been working in a large department store in Japan for five years when I decided I wanted to improve my English. And what better place to do this than in England! I chose Luton for two reasons – firstly it is an ideal base to see the rest of the country, with London only 40 minutes away. And the course is very interesting: in addition to language, you study culture as well. The most surprising thing is the amount of free time you get. OK, so you have to study, but it also allows you to go on day trips and to the movies, which all helps to improve your English.

Ruth Woodward	B

After working as an Occupational Therapist for a number of years, I realised I needed to obtain further skills to become a manager. I was advised that Luton was an ideal place to do this and did some research into their reputation – which I found to be very high. The management courses are used by many top companies and the facilities are excellent. It certainly lives up to its reputation. We are taught in small groups and you are encouraged right from the start to be active. I make contacts easily and it didn't take long before people knew my name! I was voted 'Student of the Year' in my department last year, which was very rewarding. As a direct result of doing this course I now manage services for the elderly and physically disabled for the county.

Nicholas Gaunt	C

I was out of work after serving a four-year apprenticeship as a steel engineer and saw higher education as the way to improve my chances of employment. There are so many positive things about my course – having some experience of the construction industry, I know that it's relevant; and the student mix of different ages and backgrounds provides interesting discussions. The social side of life shouldn't be overlooked either. I have made so many new friends and I also play volleyball and do weights in the university gym.

Phil Negus	D

After a time of unemployment I joined a non-degree course at the university. I really enjoyed this and it gave me the confidence to try and do a degree course at Luton. My brother really encouraged me too – he's a lecturer at Leicester University.
I have such a positive view of life now and am confident that I will fulfil my potential. Everybody should think about education and the benefits it can bring. Look at me, I have gone from being unemployed to working towards a degree and hopefully having the chance to move into my chosen career of HIV counselling or youth work.

Rebecca Stafford-Jones	E

My father is a builder and he encouraged my interest in building surveying – not the usual subject choice for a girl but after all this is the 1990s! On our programme we share lectures with students on the Construction Management course so we get a broader view of the building industry.
Out of 48 students on the course only three are girls! So in addition to studying I also have to deal with male attitudes to women in my chosen career!

Paper 2 – Writing

PART 1

You **must** answer this question.

1   You have invited a British friend of yours, who is spending a few
    months in your country, to spend some time with your family. You have
    now received the letter below from him:

> Unfortunately I have had to change some of my plans and I'm not
> going to be able to come and visit you on the weekend of the 2nd and
> 3rd. Is there any other weekend that is possible? Maybe if you don't
> have a full weekend free, I can come for a day, or one and a half days.
> Do let me know when the best time for you is. I'm really sorry about
> having to cancel the 2nd, but I am sure you will understand.
>
> Write soon and let me know.
>
> Best wishes,
>
> George

Read the letter from your friend and the diary below with the notes
you have made for yourself. Then write the letter to your friend,
suggesting suitable alternative plans for a visit.

Call M. –
George to
come too?

Extra tickets?

SATURDAY	2 GEORGE VISITING Museum?	9 Rock concert at Apollo	16 Tennis Coaching WEEKEND	23 Maria's party	30
SUNDAY	3 Excursion to Botanic Gardens?	10 Morning: English Club Meeting (film)	17 Find out if guests allowed.	24 Morning: English Club Meeting: Planning next year's activities	31

Find out which film
– George might be interested.

Write a **letter** of between **120 and 180** words in an appropriate style.
Do not write any addresses.

PART 2

Write an answer to **one** of the questions **2–5** in this part. Write your answer in **120–180** words in an appropriate style.

2   The English Club in your school has decided to put on a play. The club now needs actors and people to help behind stage. You have been asked to write a short article for your school magazine saying what the play is about, encouraging people to come and take part in it, and explaining why it would be fun to take part.

Write your **article**.

3   You have decided to enter a ghost story competition. The competition rules say that the ghost story must begin or end with the following words:

Lydia looked out of the car window and thought to herself, 'Is it never going to stop raining?'

Write your **story** for the competition.

4   You have seen the following advertisement on the board in your school:

> The George Richardson Travel Award is open to any present or past student of this school who wishes to travel to the European country of their choice, or elsewhere, in connection with their studies. Its value is about £500.
>
> APPLICATIONS, IN WRITING, TO JOHN MAYBURY WITHIN TWO WEEKS OF THIS NOTICE

You have decided to apply for the travel award advertised. Write your **application**, explaining what you would do with the money.

5   **Background reading texts**

Answer **one** of the following two questions based on your reading of **one** of the set books.

(a) Which scene in the book you have read is your favourite scene? Describe it briefly and explain why you like it more than other parts of the book.

(b) Many famous books have had sequels written for them: that is, another author writes a novel about what happened after the end of the book. Write a short summary of the plot of a sequel for the book you have read. Make sure that you describe the links between the book you have read and the sequel.

Paper 3 – Use of English

PART 1

For questions **1–15**, read the text below and decide which answer **A**, **B**, **C** or **D** best fits each space. There is an example at the beginning (**0**). Mark your answers **on the separate answer sheet**.

Example:

0 **A** counting on   **B** based on   **C** relying on   **D** according to

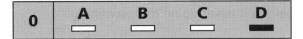

What teenagers do with their money

Thirteen-year-olds do not spend as much money as their parents suspect – at least not **(0)**..... the findings of a **(1)**..... survey, *Money and Change*. The survey **(2)**..... three hundred teenagers, 13–17 years old, from **(3)**..... Britain.

By the time they **(4)**..... their teens, most children see their weekly allowance rise dramatically to an amazing national average of £5.14. Two thirds think they get **(5)**..... money, but most expect to have to do something to get it.

Although they have more cash, worry about debt is **(6)**..... among teenagers. Therefore, the **(7)**..... of children **(8)**..... an effort to save for the future.

Greater access to cash **(9)**..... teenagers does not, however, mean that they are more irresponsible **(10)**..... a result. The economic recession seems to have encouraged **(11)**..... attitudes to money, even in the case of children at these ages. Instead of wasting what pocket **(12)**..... they have on sweets or magazines, the 13-year-olds who took **(13)**..... in the survey seem to **(14)**..... to the situation by saving more than half **(15)**..... their cash.

1 **A** late **B** recent **C** latest **D** fresh

2 **A** included **B** contained **C** counted **D** enclosed

3 **A** entire **B** all over **C** complete **D** the whole

4 **A** reach **B** get **C** make **D** arrive

5 **A** acceptable **B** adequate **C** satisfactory **D** enough

6 **A** gaining **B** heightening **C** increasing **D** building

7 **A** most **B** maximum **C** many **D** majority

8 **A** make **B** do **C** have **D** try

9 **A** among **B** through **C** between **D** along

10 **A** like **B** as **C** for **D** in

11 **A** aware **B** knowing **C** helpful **D** cautious

12 **A** cash **B** money **C** change **D** savings

13 **A** part **B** place **C** share **D** piece

14 **A** reply **B** answer **C** respond **D** return

15 **A** from **B** as **C** of **D** for

PART 2

For questions **16–30**, read the text below and think of the word which best fits each space. Use only **one** word in each space. There is an example at the beginning (**0**).
Write your word **on the separate answer sheet**.

Example:

0	*like*	**0** ___ ___

The flying wing: aeroplane of the future

What will the aeroplane of the future look **(0)**............... ? An increasing number of journeys are being made **(16)**............... air, and the airlines are therefore demanding a new kind of plane **(17)**............... help them cope with increasing passenger numbers.
(18)............... of the revolutionary new designs **(19)**............... developed is a 'flying wing', which is short but very wide, in contrast **(20)**............... most planes, which are long and narrow. It will be capable **(21)**............... carrying 600–800 passengers. It will be built of an extremely light material, and together **(22)**............... the unusual design, this will improve performance. The new aeroplane will be quieter and more comfortable

(23)............... existing planes. It will also cost less to operate, and will therefore help to keep fares **(24)**............... affordable levels.

Computers will play **(25)**............... important role in this plane. They would be used **(26)**............... the flight as **(27)**............... as on ground: ground crews will simply plug their laptop computers into the flight computers to check all functions.

An additional advantage of this plane is **(28)**............... no new runways or terminal buildings will have to be built for it, **(29)**............... it is being designed in such a way that it can **(30)**............... existing ones.

PART 3

For questions **31–40**, complete the second sentence so that it has a similar meaning to the first sentence, using the word given. **Do not change the word given.** You must use between two and five words, including the word given. There is an example at the beginning (**0**).
Write **only** the missing words **on the separate answer sheet**.

Example:

0   According to Mike, this is the best restaurant in town.
     claims
     Mike .... the best restaurant in town.

The gap can be filled by the words 'claims that this is', so you write:

| **0** | claims that this is |

31 I was never allowed to walk barefoot when I was a child.
let
My parents .... barefoot when I was a child.

32 I'm sure that her success made her parents feel wonderful.
must
Her success .... feel wonderful.

33 'I'm sorry I have to leave so early,' John said.
apologised
John .... leave so early.

34 This is the worst production of this play I have ever seen.
bad
I have .... production of this play.

35 Mary moved here in 1987.
living
Mary .... 1987.

36 I haven't decided yet whether to move or not.
mind
I haven't .... whether to move or not.

37 It is increasingly difficult for me to read without my glasses.
finding
I am .... to read without my glasses.

38 I will continue speaking only if you don't interrupt me any more.
stop
I will continue speaking only .... me.

39 Can you tell me what she looks like?
describe
Can .... me?

40 They have been telling him that he should apply for this job.
encouraging
They have been .... for this job.

PART 4

For questions **41–55**, read the text below and look carefully at each line. Some of the lines are correct, and some have a word which should not be there.

If a line is correct put a tick (✓) by the number **on the separate answer sheet**. If a line has a word which should **not** be there, write the word **on the separate answer sheet**. There are two examples at the beginning (**0** and **00**).

Examples:

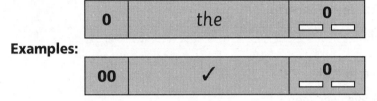

0	the	0
00	✓	0

Living in London

0	'When a man is tired of London, he is tired of the life.'
00	From my own experience, this saying of the 18th
41	century writer, Dr Johnson, is definitely right: London
42	has a lot to offer. When I was first arrived in London
43	for to study English, I thought that I would spend most
44	of my spare time in studying. But very soon I was going
45	out on every evening, either to the theatre or to jazz
46	clubs (because that London has many famous clubs).
47	My weekends were also full: I would go to sports
48	events, to exhibitions, or just wander around. I used to
49	joke that I was renting a room that I wasn't spending
50	any time in it! Luckily, I also realised that I was not
51	studying enough and started staying at home more, and
52	studying much more harder. I learnt that you should
53	never feel that you must to do everything that is
54	available. Still, I am sure that if you ever visit in
55	London, you will agree with what Dr Johnson had said.

PART 5

For questions **56–65**, read the text below. Use the word given in capitals at the end of each line to form a word that fits in the space in the same line. There is an example at the beginning **(0)**. Write your word **on the separate answer sheet**.

Example:

0	*exceptional*	0 __ __

Genius

We all know stories about people with **(0)**.............. memories who have the   **EXCEPTION**

(56).............. to remember hundreds of numbers after hearing them only   **ABLE**

once. Now experts are saying that such feats can be taught.

For example, most people can **(57)**.............. about nine numbers if they are read   **REPETITION**

out one a second. In one experiment, ten hours' training **(58)**.............. only a   **PRODUCT**

small **(59)**.............. , but the results after practising for a thousand hours were   **IMPROVE**

(60).............. : some people remembered 80 or even 100 numbers. Similarly,   **AMAZE**

most adults can **(61)**.............. only about five out of a set of 21 colours that are   **IDENTITY**

only **(62)**.............. different. But after 80 training hours one person could   **SLIGHT**

recognise 18 of them. Studies of 76 major **(63)**.............. show that it took at   **COMPOSE**

least ten years of **(64)**.............. training before any of them wrote a major work.   **MUSIC**

Psychologists are therefore raising the **(65)**.............. that genius is the product   **POSSIBLE**

of teaching.

Paper 4 – Listening

PART 1

You will hear people talking in eight different situations.
For questions **1–8**, choose the best answer, **A**, **B** or **C**.

1   Listen to this woman apologising for being late. Why was she late?
    A   There was an accident.
    B   She took the wrong bus.
    C   The bus broke down.

    [ ] 1

2   You are sitting in a travel office when you hear a man talking to the travel agent. Why is the man changing his flight?
    A   The original flight was cancelled.
    B   He is looking for a cheaper flight.
    C   He has to return earlier than he thought.

    [ ] 2

3   You are sitting in a university cafeteria and overhear a man speaking. What does the man think about his boss's last decision?
    A   He agrees with it.
    B   He disagrees with it.
    C   He has no opinion about it.

    [ ] 3

4   Listen to these two friends talking. Where are they?
    A   At an airport.
    B   At a train station.
    C   At a bus station.

    [ ] 4

5   You are walking past a large hall when you hear a man talking. Who is the man talking to?
    A   A group of actors.
    B   An orchestra.
    C   A group of singers.

    [ ] 5

6   You are in a shop when you hear this conversation. What is the woman doing?
    A   Apologising.
    B   Asking a question.
    C   Making a request.

    [ ] 6

7   Listen to this answerphone message. What is the relationship between the speaker and Mary?
    A   They know each other very well and are good friends.
    B   They are on good terms, but are not really friends.
    C   Their relationship is basically only a work relationship.

    [ ] 7

8   Listen to this woman speaking about her schooldays. Who is she talking about?
    A   A school teacher.
    B   Her father.
    C   Another student.

    [ ] 8

PART 2

You will hear a woman talking to a grocer ordering food to be delivered to her house.
For questions **9–18**, complete the notes.

Customer: | | **9**

Order: | | **10**

| | **11**

Total to pay: | | **12**

Method of payment: | | **13**

Deliver together with: | | **14**

Time of delivery: | | **15**

Address: 21, Swainstone Road

How to get there –

after roundabout, take | | **16**

Next week deliver on | | **17**

instead of on | | **18**

PART 3

You will hear five different people talking about parking cars. They are answering the question: should learner drivers take a parking test?
For questions **19–23**, choose from the list **A–F** the description that suits each person. Use the letters only once. There is one extra letter which you do not need to use.

A   This speaker claims driving tests are too difficult anyway.

B   This speaker had a minor accident while learning to drive.

C   This speaker says men are better parkers than women.

D   This speaker says that other people can pressure you into making mistakes.

E   This speaker mentions economic reasons against including parking in the test.

F   This speaker failed the test a number of times before passing.

Speaker 1		19
Speaker 2		20
Speaker 3		21
Speaker 4		22
Speaker 5		23

PART 4

You will hear an interview with a young couple talking about where they live.

For questions **24–30**, decide which of the choices **A**, **B** or **C** is the correct answer.

24 The Jacksons went to live

    A abroad.
    B in the suburbs.
    C in the country.

            24

25 The Jacksons are living

    A in a rented house.
    B with Carol's mother.
    C in a house they bought.

            25

26 Carol says that

    A it is very important to have a great deal of parking space.
    B she likes living in a peaceful and safe place.
    C the children enjoy sleeping in the car.

            26

27 What do the Jacksons say about farm life?

    A They don't really like farming.
    B They have made a number of mistakes.
    C Their children hate eating only vegetables.

            27

28 Why do the Jacksons have to bring water in containers?

    A The water is not healthy enough for drinking.
    B They have no water supply.
    C They prefer drinking bottled water.

            28

29 What do the Jacksons feel about their house?

    A They complain about the hardships.
    B They enjoy having electricity.
    C They love living simply.

            29

30 What do the Jacksons say about the local community?

    A They feel they are well established there.
    B The local community has rejected them.
    C They still don't feel totally accepted.

            30

Paper 5 – Speaking

The photographs and pictures the interlocutor refers to appear on pages 114–116.

PART 1

The interlocutor encourages each of the candidates in turn to give personal information about themselves by asking questions such as:

Where are you from?
How long have you lived here/there?
What is it like living here/there?
How do you usually spend your free time?
What are your plans for the future?

PART 2

The interlocutor gives each of the candidates in turn two photographs to look at and gives the following instructions:

Candidate A, here are your two pictures. Please let Candidate B see them. They show two different bedrooms. Candidate A, I'd like you to compare and contrast these pictures saying how you feel about bedrooms like these. When Candidate A has finished, I'd like you, Candidate B, to tell us which bedroom you would choose for yourself if you could.

* * *

Candidate B, here are your two pictures. Please let Candidate A see them. They show different people going on holiday. Candidate B, I'd like you to compare and contrast these pictures saying how you feel about situations like these. When Candidate B has finished, I'd like you, Candidate A, to tell us which of these two ways to travel you would choose if you were going on holiday.

PART 3

The interlocutor gives the candidates some illustrations to look at and gives the following instructions:

Now, Candidates A and B, here are a number of pictures which people have suggested could be hung in different rooms in a language school. Choose the three pictures which could go into the reception area, cafeteria and a classroom in the school.

PART 4

The interlocutor encourages the candidates to develop the topic raised in Part 3 by asking questions such as:

Is the way in which a room is decorated important?
How is your room decorated?
Who decides on the decoration of the rooms in your house?
In your school, do you have posters on the walls in the classes? And in the corridors?
If so, do they contribute to the atmosphere? If not, would you prefer to have posters, etc. on the walls?

Practice exam 2

Paper 1 – Reading

PART 1

You are going to read a magazine article describing different types of exercises. Below are nine drawings. Eight of them have been taken out of the instructions. For questions **1–7**, decide which of the drawings **A–I** belongs in each gap. There is one extra drawing which you do not need to use. Each drawing should illustrate the exercise described below it. There is an example at the beginning (**0**).
Mark your answers **on the separate answer sheet**.

0 | **I**

To stretch your calves and keep your ankles mobile: stand facing a wall, at arm's length. Place your hands on the wall for support and stretch your right leg out straight behind you, the ball of your foot on the floor, your toes pointing at the wall. Gently push your right heel towards the floor, allowing your left leg to bend as shown.

1

To stretch the muscles in your shoulders, trunk and legs: stand tall and relaxed. Stretching through your whole body, reach up towards the ceiling with your fingertips. Then, letting yourself bend at the hips and the knees, slowly bring your hands down towards the floor, as far as is comfortable. Straighten up and repeat.

2

For supple shoulders: start with your arms at your sides, hips facing forwards: circle your right arm forward, up and back. Repeat with your left arm; continue on alternate sides.

3

To keep your hips mobile and stretch the thigh muscles: stand tall and relaxed, your weight on your left leg. Rest your left hand on a chair for support. Swing your right leg forwards and back in a relaxed, pendulum action. Gradually take your leg as high as you comfortably can, keeping your body fairly upright and letting your right knee bend. Repeat with the left leg.

4

To stretch your lower back and the backs of your thighs: sit on the floor, your legs straight in front of you, your knees as near the floor as is comfortable. Place your hands on your thighs. Slowly slide your hands down your legs as far as you can comfortably reach. Return to the upright position and repeat. Do not bounce into the movement.

5

To stretch your side muscles and help keep your spine flexible: stand tall and relaxed, feet apart, hands at your sides. Slowly bend to the left and right alternately, allowing your hands to slide down your legs. Make sure you are bending sideways; don't let your shoulders drop forwards. Stand tall between bends. Keep the legs straight.

6

To restore energy: stand upright, your back straight, feet slightly apart. Slowly let your chin drop onto your chest, continuing this downward motion until you round your back and your arms fall gently towards your feet. When you have reached as far as you can, relax, and hold for a full minute. Slowly straighten up and repeat three times.

7

To restore energy: stand upright, your feet slightly apart, arms at your side. Use your right arm to rub your left arm vigorously, and vice versa. Then bend forward and use both hands to rub each leg. Finish by shaking your hands and feet. Now you're ready to go!

PART 2

You are going to read a text about Michael Marks, one of the founders of the famous British store, Marks and Spencer's. For questions **8–14**, choose the answer (**A, B, C** or **D**) which you think fits best according to the text. Mark your answers **on the separate answer sheet**.

The Birth of the Penny Bazaar

From the open market in Leeds, Michael Marks moved to its covered market hall, which had the advantage of giving protection against the weather and of being open for trading
5 throughout the week. Here he soon introduced an innovation which was to be of fundamental importance to the development of his business. He divided his stall into two sections, and placed all those items costing a
10 penny in one section and all those costing more in the other, where the prices were individually marked. Above the penny section hung a board with the words: 'Don't Ask the Price. It's a Penny.'

15 This proved to be one of the most successful advertising slogans ever invented. It was not only striking and simple and easily understood; it also answered a genuine popular need. Michael Marks's customers came
20 from the working-class, then largely illiterate, and were keen to satisfy their domestic needs at a low price; the combination of open display, easy inspection, and a fixed price made shopping easy and convenient for them.
25 'Don't Ask the Price. It's a Penny' quickly proved so popular that Michael Marks adopted the principle of the fixed price on all his stalls and from that moment on sold nothing that cost more than a penny.

30 The success of this new way of selling was extremely important for the development of the business. It proved not only to be convenient to the customer, it was also extremely convenient to the stall owner.

35 Michael Marks never kept any accounts, and conducted his business operation by mental arithmetic; adopting a single fixed price of a penny made his calculations much simpler. This element of operational simplicity was to
40 become a central feature of the business. It was, in fact, a revolution: Michael Marks had discovered and put into practice two simple ideas – self-selection and self-service – which were to become cardinal principles in selling in
45 the second half of the twentieth century.

In shops at this time, which were often small and dark, it was still usual to keep goods in drawers under the counter or on shelves behind it. You had to ask for everything
50 before you even saw if it was there. However, many people are shy of going into shops; sometimes they even avoid it, in case they show their ignorance, or for fear that shopkeepers, or shop assistants, might look
55 down on them or exploit them. This did not happen when people came to shop with Michael Marks. They could walk around Michael's penny bazaar without being pushed to buy. They were at ease.

60 The adoption of fixed prices had also another far-reaching effect. It meant that Michael Marks had to search for as wide a variety of goods as possible, and of as high a quality as possible, that could be sold for a penny; as a
65 result he had to accept that the profit on each item would be low, and make up for this by selling as many items as possible.

8 According to the text

    A the open air market was not a successful place.

    B the open air market was not open every day.

    C more people came to the open air market.

    D selling at a fixed price was only possible indoors.

9 What was the reason for Marks's success?

    A His goods were much better than anyone else's.

    B He was never rude to customers.

    C He made all his calculations in his head.

    D He made shopping easy.

10 Michael Marks is portrayed as a man who

    A was very bad at doing arithmetic.

    B revolutionised selling methods.

    C didn't understand working-class people.

    D read a lot about business methods.

11 According to the text, why did some people not like buying in shops?

    A Prices were often too high in shops.

    B They didn't like discussing what they would buy.

    C They didn't feel at ease with the shop assistants.

    D In the market they could buy a greater range of goods.

12 The word 'cardinal' in line 44 means

    A important.

    B religious.

    C impressive.

    D urgent.

13 The word 'this' in line 66 refers to

    A the low profits for each item.

    B the need for high-quality goods.

    C the need for low-price items.

    D selling as many items as possible.

14 Where is this text from?

    A A training manual for shop assistants.

    B An advertisement for Marks and Spencer's products.

    C A book about the history of Leeds.

    D A book about business methods.

PART 3

You are going to read a newspaper article about the manager of a children's museum. Seven paragraphs have been removed from the article. Choose from the paragraphs **A–H** the one which fits each gap (**15–20**). There is one extra paragraph which you do not need to use. There is an example at the beginning (**0**).
Mark your answers **on the separate answer sheet**.

MAKING FUN OF EDUCATION
Britain's first national children's museum aims to change the idea that learning is boring.

Gillian Thomas admits she is one of the lucky people who are so interested in their work that they find it difficult to separate it from play. 'I'd rather be doing my job than playing tennis,' she says.

0	H

Ms Thomas enjoyed school and Oxford university, although teaching secondary-school chemistry in London was less exciting. 'It felt too easy, round and round the same thing.'

15	

She says she is still learning, still finding things fascinating, a philosophy she hopes Eureka will pass on to the 500,000 visitors it expects to attract annually within three years of opening. 'Using your hands and exploring with your senses is a way to get people to think,' she says. 'We are trying to create an environment where learning through play can continue. I want a trip to Eureka to be thoroughly satisfying, amusing but also serious and absorbing.'

16	

The choice of Halifax was influenced by the Prince of Wales. When he and the Princess of Wales were asked to become patrons of the museum, they agreed on condition it was built in the north.

17	

Research into children's interests and perceptions is already under way. She started with banking. 'Frankly, we thought it was the most boring, and so we thought we'd start with the difficult one.'

18	

She admits to learning a lot from her own children. Her son Caspar is studying astrophysics at Cornell University in New York, and her daughter Hope has been taking A-level French and Art.

19	

Before Halifax Ms Thomas lived in Paris. She learnt French at the Sorbonne, at the same time teaching science in English to French children. She then spent seven years at La Villette, the city for science and industry.

20	

'It's relatively rare for someone to span the whole range from ideas to development, through the building stage, to the up and running,' she says. 'I liked the idea of trying to adapt that experience to a different situation in Halifax.'

A To do that she plans three exhibitions for the opening: 'Living and Working Together', showing how a town works; 'You and Your Body', exploring what makes everyone individual; and 'Inventing and Creating', which will include exhibitions of failed and successful inventions.

B 'It's an area with a fascinating history in terms of invention,' Ms Thomas says. 'It is a very different feel from the south.'

C The idea for Eureka received the backing of Vivien Duffield, the chairperson of the Vivien Duffield Foundation. She, too, had been impressed by a visit to the children's museum in Boston.

D When her own two children were young, she worked at home running a company making kites. She then returned to studying, obtaining a master's degree in science education.

E Not so. Children were fascinated by the idea of money. When one group were asked what a bank manager does, half sat back and put their feet on the desk.

F For one year after Caspar was born, she did nothing except watch him closely, thinking how to stimulate him. 'I was hovering to spot the next time he moved to see what I could offer him as a stimulating experience,' she says. 'I soon realised I needed a wider field in which to use my energies.'

G Her suggestions to the team for the La Villette project brought her the offer of a job. She joined the team as science adviser to the children's centre before being placed in charge. She soon headed the youth department, and the decision was taken to double the size of the children's centre. That was before Eureka came along.

H Ms Thomas is the director of Eureka, Britain's first national children's museum, which is under construction in Halifax, West Yorkshire. Eureka, she says, will attempt to push back the moment when children say: 'Education is boring. I don't want any more of it.'

PART 4

You are going to read an excerpt from a newspaper in which seven journalists describe what they would do if they were given £30,000. For questions **21–35** choose from the list of people (**A–G**). Some of the people may be chosen more than once. When more than one answer is required, these may be given in any order. There is an example at the beginning (**0**).
Mark your answers **on the separate answer sheet**.

Which of the journalists:

would write a travel book?	**0**	E	
would go on writing for the newspaper?	**21**		
would buy a car?	**22**	**23**	
would study?	**24**	**25**	
cannot drive?	**26**		
criticises the way they were brought up?	**27**		
would write a biography?	**28**		
would open a kind of hotel?	**29**		
complains about their present job?	**30**		
would go abroad and travel?	**31**	**32**	
regrets not doing something in the past?	**33**		
has written a humorous answer?	**34**		
is worried about making a wrong decision in the future?	**35**		

Independent staff members say how their lives would change were they to receive an award of £30,000.

Father's footsteps: Christian Wolmar   A

My father was born in Russia. He commanded an army unit in 1916, and was imprisoned by the Bolsheviks. He fled to Paris and later to New York and came to London in 1937. I have written down his memoirs from tapes which describe his life, but for this to be enough for a book, I need to visit the Moscow streets where he spent his childhood, follow his path during the Revolution, and see where he lived in Paris and New York. I need the money for this and to live on while I am writing the book.

Breaking out: Catherine Tennant   B

Growing up isolated in the Lake District, in north-west England, I relied on my father's driving to maintain contact with friends and shops. I was totally controlled – spontaneous visits were out of the question. My mother hated English traffic and gave up her licence. Having seen her dependence on my father, I should have learnt my lesson. But I was scared. Now I live in London and lie to myself that I don't need to drive, forgetting that my inability has lost me several jobs. With £30,000 I could have driving lessons, buy a car, drive to the Lake District and drive my mother from lake to lake.

Follow your heart: Justin Keeryh   C

I met an American girl at Chicago airport last summer. We fell in love and crossed the Atlantic seven times in the past year. We almost got married, but didn't have the courage to do it after only a few visits. £30,000 would be enough to get me through a degree course in the university where she teaches. In that time we will either find out that we need to get married, or be able to stop worrying that we've thrown away something wonderful.

Moving abroad: Patrick Miles   D

I would buy a small farm on the coast in Kenya. With a little help from some of the local lads I know, I would build a house and a few simple huts to rent to travellers. I would grow fruit and vegetables, buy a fishing boat, and send short articles back home. Mainly about politics.

Hit the road: Jason Nissé   E

If I had £30,000, I would go to America, buy a convertible and drive it everywhere from Alaska to Guatemala, from the Atlantic to the Pacific. I would eat at cheap restaurants, and sleep in the car if I couldn't find a motel to sleep in. I would spend a year writing down my thoughts in a notebook which I would try and turn into a best-selling book when I returned home. And at the end of the year, I would simply go back to work. Refreshed.

Back in control: Deidre Kingsman   F

£30,000 would give me freedom, control and therefore joy. I would leave my job immediately, and first rest for a month to get my body clock back to normal after years of shift-work. Then I would take a course in film and animation, as this is the one activity where, for me, work and pleasure would be one and the same.

Cameras roll: James Donald   G

I would do something down to earth, modest and useful: become a movie star. I wouldn't go to film school – I don't want to do any work – but buy myself a role in the latest movie being made, just a little part to get me noticed by other directors. Then the bright lights of Hollywood would call me and I would run to them. When I started earning millions, I would do lots of unselfish and charitable things with my money. Honest.

Paper 2 – Writing

PART 1

You **must** answer this question.

1   You have seen the advertisement below and have decided that you are
    interested in taking part in the experiment described. Using the
    advertisement and the notes you have made below it, write a letter
    covering the points in the advertisement and in your notes.

Research on Eating Habits

We are looking for students willing to take part in an experiment on
eating habits. The survey will last three weeks. You will be asked to
have lunch and dinner three times a week at the Food Science
Department, and keep a record of your other meals.

A small fee will be paid.

If you are interested, please write to Dr. S. D. Allan, Dept. of Food
Science, stating your preferred days for the experiment.

We also need to know what your present eating habits are so please
include information about how many times a day you eat, the type of
food you eat, whether you eat between meals, etc.

---

meals – free?
fee – how much?
when start?
choice of food or fixed meal?

Write a **letter** of between **120 and 180** words in an appropriate style.
Do not write any addresses.

PART 2

Write an answer to **one** of the questions **2–5** in this part. Write your answer in **120–180** words in an appropriate style.

2   You have seen this letter in an English-language newspaper:

Dear Sir,

Young people today watch too much television. When I was a child, we played games, developing friendships. We read, developing our knowledge of languages. We had active hobbies: stamp collecting, bird watching. Today, youngsters sit passively and watch the rubbish on the television screen. No wonder educational standards are falling!

Yours faithfully,

J. Row

Write a **letter** to the editor expressing your opinion about what the writer of this letter says. Do not write any addresses.

3   You have decided to enter a short story competition. The story must begin or end with the words:

Mary rushed down the stairs, laughing happily. In her hand she was holding the letter for which she had been waiting for so long.

Write your **story** for the competition.

4   You have started working for a company which is interested in opening a large music store (selling equipment, records, cassettes and CDs) in your town. You have been asked to produce a report describing which music shops exist in your town and other towns in the area, what these shops are like, and where people shop for music and musical equipment.

Write your **report**.

5   **Background reading texts**

Answer **one** of the following two questions based on your reading of **one** of the set books.

(a) Describe the setting of the book you read. In what way does the setting contribute to the plot or to other aspects of the book?

(b) Your class has decided to make a short video film out of the book you have read, and you have been asked to direct it. Write a **letter** to the producer of the film telling him or her which of your classmates or friends you have chosen for the lead roles, and explain why. Do not write any addresses.

Paper 3 – Use of English

PART 1

For questions **1–15**, read the text below and decide which answer **A, B, C** or **D** best fits each space. There is an example at the beginning (**0**).
Mark your answers **on the separate answer sheet**.

Example:

0 **A** realism   **B** realisation   **C** reality   **D** realist

0	A	B	C	D
	▭	▭	▬	▭

Becoming a nurse: the interview

The **(0)**..... of an interview is never as bad as your fears. For some **(1)**..... people imagine the interviewer is going to jump on every tiny mistake they **(2)**..... . In truth, the interviewer is as **(3)**..... for the meeting to go well as you are. It is what **(4)**..... his or her job enjoyable.

The secret of a good interview is preparing for it. What you wear is always important as it creates the first impression. So **(5)**..... neatly, but comfortably. Make **(6)**..... that you can deal with anything you are **(7)**..... . Prepare for questions that are certain to come up, for example: Why do you want to become a nurse? What is the most important **(8)**..... a good nurse should have? Apart from nursing, what other careers have you **(9)**.....? What are your interests and hobbies?

Answer the questions fully and precisely. **(10)**..... , if one of your interests is reading, be prepared to **(11)**..... about the sort of books you like. **(12)**..... , do not learn all your answers off **(13)**..... heart. The interviewer wants to meet a human **(14)**..... , not a robot. Remember, the interviewer is genuinely interested in you, so the more you relax and are yourself, the more **(15)**..... you are to succeed.

1	**A**	reason	**B**	idea	**C**	explanation	**D**	excuse
2	**A**	perform	**B**	do	**C**	make	**D**	have
3	**A**	keen	**B**	wanting	**C**	interested	**D**	delighted
4	**A**	does	**B**	causes	**C**	happens	**D**	makes
5	**A**	dress	**B**	wear	**C**	put on	**D**	have on
6	**A**	evident	**B**	sure	**C**	definite	**D**	clear
7	**A**	requested	**B**	questioned	**C**	enquired	**D**	asked
8	**A**	character	**B**	quality	**C**	nature	**D**	point

9	A	thought	B	regarded	C	considered	D	wondered
10	A	For instance	B	That is	C	Such as	D	Let's say
11	A	say	B	talk	C	discuss	D	chat
12	A	However	B	Although	C	Despite	D	Therefore
13	A	at	B	in	C	on	D	by
14	A	character	B	being	C	somebody	D	nature
15	A	easy	B	possible	C	likely	D	probable

PART 2

For questions **16–30**, read the text below and think of the word which best fits each space. Use only one word in each space. There is an example at the beginning (**0**).
Write your word **on the separate answer sheet**.

Example:

0	one	0

Gang thought Bruegel was rubbish

Many stolen paintings have a strange history. But **(0)**......... of the strangest was that of a painting by the famous sixteenth-century painter Bruegel, stolen from the Courtauld Institute in London in the Eighties. It had fallen **(16)**............... the hands of four thieves in London, **(17)**............... were trying to **(18)**.............. a quick profit. Until they showed the painting to an art expert, **(19)**............... , they had no idea how much it was worth. One of **(20)**.............. said: 'We got this old chap to come in and **(21)**.............. a look at the painting. He was talking about something, then turned **(22)**............... , saw the painting and fainted. So I thought it was probably valuable.'

Two months later, the gang telephoned **(23)**.............. art expert. This expert told them that the painting was worth £2–3 million. They immediately hung up. They then tried to sell the painting back to the gallery from **(24)**............... it had been stolen. The gallery contacted the police and a meeting **(25)**............... arranged. The gang asked **(26)**............... the money to be brought in two suitcases in unmarked banknotes. **(27)**............... the meeting did in fact take place, the deal fell through and no money changed hands.

A short **(28)**............... later the four were arrested. The police found the painting on **(29)**............... of a wardrobe. When the gang were told they were **(30)**............... arrested in connection with the Bruegel, one of them said: 'What's a Bruegel? I thought it was rubbish.'

PART 3

For questions **31–40,** complete the second sentence so that is has a similar meaning to the first sentence, using the word given. **Do not change the word given.** You must use between two and five words, including the word given. There is an example at the beginning (**0**).
Write **only** the missing words **on the separate answer sheet.**

Example:

0 They discussed the new proposals at length.
   long
   They .... about the new proposals.

The gap can be filled by the words 'had a long discussion', so you write:

0	had a long discussion

31 The person who encouraged me the most at school was my French teacher.
   encouragement
   The person who .... at school was my French teacher.

32 I found this film quite disappointing.
   let
   I felt quite .... film.

33 The play was so boring that we left in the interval.
   so
   We were .... that we left in the interval.

34 'Mark, could you write up the report immediately?' Peter said.
   wanted
   Peter told Mark .... write up the report immediately.

35 Please don't go there now.
   rather
   I .... go there now.

36 I probably forgot to mention that the deadline is Tuesday.
   may
   I .... that the deadline is Tuesday.

37 I last heard this song ten years ago.
   been
   It .... I last heard this song.

38 Please don't stop your work.
   carry
   Please .... your work.

40

39 This office is too small for two people.
   enough
   This office .... for two people.

40 'Could you wait a second while I get my books?' George asked Bridget.
   asked
   George .... a second while he got his books.

PART 4

For questions **41–55,** read the text below and look carefully at each line. Some of the lines are correct, and some have a word which should not be there.
If a line is correct, put a tick (✓) by the number **on the separate answer sheet**. If a line has a word which should **not** be there, write the word **on the separate answer sheet**. There are two examples at the beginning (**0** and **00**).

Examples:

0	✓	0

00	was	0

An unlucky day

0 Last Sunday was definitely not a good day for me. It
00 was all started when I got into my car and it refused
41 to start. I immediately realised that I had left the
42 lights on and the battery had gone flat. I telephoned to
43 my friend George and he came round and helped me
44 start the car. I then drove into town to see a friend. I
45 had arranged to meet him at six and thirty, but by
46 the time I got to there, it was ten past seven and my
47 friend he was not there. I waited for him for an hour
48 despite of the freezing weather, but he didn't come.
49 When I had returned to my car, I saw that someone
50 had been broken into it, probably looking for the radio.
51 Luckily, I never leave the radio in the car! There
52 was nothing I could do but get into my car and drive to home.
53 Later I spoke with my friend and discovered out that he
54 had waited for only the half an hour and left. He didn't
55 even apologise himself for not waiting for me longer!

PART 5

For questions **56–65**, read the text below. Use the word given in capitals at the end of each line to form a word that fits in the space in the same line. There is an example at the beginning (**0**). Write your word **on the separate answer sheet**.

Example:

0	proud	0 __ __

Healthy eating

In the past, any mother would be (**0**)............... if her children were round   **PRIDE**

and slightly fat. Those days are gone. (**56**)............... have now reached   **RESEARCH**

the (**57**)............... that too much fat and sugar in children's diets are a   **CONCLUDE**

major factor in the (**58**)............... of heart diseases and other   **DEVELOP**

(**59**)............... when they are older.   **ILL**

However, (**60**)............... children need to eat a wide range of foods, and   **GROW**

their general health could be (**61**)............... by cutting out particular ones.   **DANGER**

Psychologists say that the (**62**)............... is not to change eating habits too   **SOLVE**

fast, but to do it (**63**)............... , so that children do not lose muscle in addition   **CARE**

to fat. Parents should present food a little (**64**)............... , spread butter thinly   **DIFFERENCE**

and avoid putting sugar on the table. Children should also be (**65**)............... to   **COURAGE**

take part in sports: this way they will be using the calories that they have eaten.

Paper 4 – Listening

PART 1

You will hear people talking in eight different situations.
For questions **1–8**, choose the best answer, **A**, **B** or **C**.

1 Listen to this man talking on the telephone and discussing the time for an inspection. When is the inspection going to take place?
  A In the afternoon.
  B In the morning.
  C At any time during the day.

1

2 You are sitting in a reception office in a school when you overhear this conversation between a man and the receptionist. The man is
  A disappointed.
  B ill.
  C relieved.

2

3 You are listening to the local radio when you hear this announcement. Why are the roads closed?
  A Because of a sports event.
  B Because of roadworks.
  C Because of an accident.

3

4 Listen to these two women discussing a common acquaintance, Margaret. What is Margaret's profession?
  A An accountant.
  B A teacher.
  C A doctor.

4

5 Listen to these people discussing their food. Where are they eating?
  A At home.
  B In a cafeteria.
  C In a restaurant.

5

6 Listen to this man talk about his childhood. What does he think about his father's behaviour?
  A He understands it.
  B He doesn't think it was right.
  C He is still angry about it.

6

7 You are walking on the street and hear a man talking. Who is he talking to?
  A Someone looking for a house to buy.
  B A group of architecture students.
  C Children living in the neighbourhood.

7

8 You are visiting friends when one of their flatmates comes into the room. The man is
  A worried.
  B formal.
  C rude.

8

43

PART 2

You will hear part of a talk about an international student organisation.
For questions **9–18**, complete the notes which summarise what the speaker
says. You will need to write a word or a short phrase in each box.

Most students in the world belong to their

	9

ISIC proves that

	10

and it it is accepted

	11

Two important advantages of ISIC are

a. you can fly

	12

b. you can use the organisation's

	13

You get a free copy of

	14

The offices can give you a list of

	15

Helpline – important if you need

	16

When you go to join, bring

	17

and

	18

PART 3

You will hear five different people talking about parties they went to. For questions **19–23**, choose from the list **A–F** which party each person went to. Use the letters only once. There is one extra letter which you do not need to use.

A   This was a wedding reception.

B   This was a party for children.

C   This was an unplanned party.

D   This is a party held at the end of a course.

E   This was a birthday party.

F   This party had a number of small accidents.

Speaker 1		19
Speaker 2		20
Speaker 3		21
Speaker 4		22
Speaker 5		23

PART 4

You will hear a conversation between three people who are planning a party, Jill, Andrew and Don.

Answer questions **24–30**, by writing   **J**   (for Jill)
                                           A   (for Andrew)
                     or   **D**   (for Don).

24   Who makes a suggestion everyone agrees with?   **| 24 |**

25   Who has just moved to the area?   **| 25 |**

26   Who makes fun of someone else?   **| 26 |**

27   Who thinks the house is too small?   **| 27 |**

28   Who is afraid that the party will be too noisy?   **| 28 |**

29   Who loses patience?   **| 29 |**

30   Who takes charge of the planning in general?   **| 30 |**

45

Paper 5 – Speaking

The photographs and pictures the interlocutor refers to appear on pages 117–119.

PART 1

The interlocutor encourages each of the candidates in turn to give personal information about themselves by asking questions such as:

Where are you from?
How long have you lived here/there?
What is it like living here/there?
How do you usually spend your free time?
What are your plans for the future?

PART 2

The interlocutor gives each of the candidates in turn two photographs to look at and gives the following instructions:

Candidate A, here are your two pictures. Please let Candidate B see them. They show two different cities. Candidate A, I'd like you to compare and contrast these pictures saying how you feel about cities like these. When Candidate A has finished, I'd like you, Candidate B, to tell us which city you would choose to live in if you had the choice.

* * *

Candidate B, here are your two pictures. Please let Candidate A see them. They show people studying in two different situations. Candidate B, I'd like you to compare and contrast these pictures saying how you feel about situations like these. When Candidate B has finished, I'd like you, Candidate A, to tell us which situation you would prefer to be in if you had a choice.

PART 3

The interlocutor gives the candidates some photographs to look at and gives the following instructions:

Now, Candidates A and B, imagine that you are abroad together and are going to visit a friend for a day. Your friend has made a number of suggestions for an outing and has asked you to indicate which three of the suggestions shown in the photographs you would prefer.

PART 4

The interlocutor encourages the candidates to develop the topic raised in Part 3 by asking questions such as:

What do you do at the weekend?
Do you ever go to places like those shown in the photographs in your own country?
Do you think people take part in the same leisure activities when they go away on holiday as they do when they are at home?
In what way would such activities be different?

Practice exam 3

Paper 1 – Reading

PART 1

You are going to read an article about twins. Choose from the list **A–H** the most suitable summary sentence for each part (**1–6**) of the article. There is one extra summary sentence which you do not need to use. There is an example at the beginning (**0**).
Mark your answers **on the separate answer sheet**.

A   You will usually find that twins are not exactly alike.

B   It has been discovered that twins who have grown up apart sometimes have amazingly similar life histories.

C   It is not clear to what degree parents should bring out the similarities between twins.

D   Studies into life histories of twins show that being a twin can lead to a very difficult life.

E   The lives of one pair of twins show extraordinary similarities.

F   Being twins has both advantages and disadvantages.

G   Managing with twins can be extremely difficult.

H   The ideas that most of us have about twins may be wrong.

DOUBLE TROUBLE FOR TWO OF A KIND

Studies into twins and their development are throwing new light on their connectedness. John Illman reports.

0	H

For years the problems of parents like Desmond and Karen Monk have been largely unrecognised in Britain. The Monks have twins: Colleen and Emily, aged five, who are the public image of twins. See them, and you see why no mother can walk with twins along the street without attracting admiring sounds from everybody. But the popular view does not recognise that beginning life as a twin, often under severe conditions, can mean special problems for parents, teachers and doctors – not to mention twins themselves.

1	

The Monks pride themselves on the way they have managed, but Karen admits: 'Things were really tough when they were aged between one and a half and three. They were just very demanding, both of them wanting your attention at the same time. If you had one on your lap, the other wanted to be there. You can't develop the same kind of one-to-one relationship with twins as you have with one child.'

2	

Twins often find great strength and support in one another. But this strong connection, endearing though it can be, can push individuality aside. The characters of individual children can be buried within one another.

3	

Despite all the similarities there are always differences. In the case of the Monks, one twin tends to be more outgoing than the other. 'When they were little, this tended to flow from one to the other. For six months one would be outgoing and the other would be the opposite, very dependent. Then they would change roles. I can't explain why.'

4	

All twin parents face a problem as to how far to play up or down twinship. Should twins have twin-like names, as has always been common practice? Should they be dressed the same to emphasise their relationship, or differently, to make it less obvious? Should they be encouraged to play together or apart? Should they go to the same school?

5	

Twins are now attracting increasing interest from scientists. Some extremely interesting research in the USA shows that even if identical twins are separated early in life and grow up in different places, they tend to develop surprising similarities.

6	

The so-called 'Jim Twins' are one example. In January 1979 James Lewis, a security guard in Lima, Ohio, found his twin brother, whom he had not seen since they were both adopted into different families at the age of five. A meeting was arranged 39 years after the twins had last seen each other. It turned out that both were called James. Both had married women called Linda, divorced and re-married, both marrying women called Betty. Both had owned dogs as boys, and called them Toy. The brothers have the same sleeping problems and share the same smoking habits. They also share 'tension headaches' that begin in the afternoon and develop into migraines.

PART 2

You are going to read a text about women who ride mountain bikes.
For questions **7–13**, choose the answer (**A, B, C,** or **D**) which you think fits
best according to the text.
Mark your answers **on the separate answer sheet**.

THE PAST few years have seen quite an increased interest by women in off-road riding. A good 15 percent of our female members ride off-road, and mountain bikes
5 seem to be gaining in popularity as a means to this end. In an effort to learn why, earlier this year readers of this column were invited to write in about their experience.

The most frequently mentioned reason for
10 trying a mountain bike was that a world existed out there that was waiting to be explored, but walking provided limited possibilities, and light touring bikes weren't felt to be tough enough for the job. Some
15 began by way of hiring one or borrowing someone else's while on holiday. For others it was a husband, a father, a daughter or a 'mad friend' that got them started. One woman claimed she would never have seen much of
20 her husband if she hadn't started riding a mountain bike!

Only about half had ridden with a group consisting of women only, but their experiences were strongly recommended.
25 Overall it was regarded as a positive and healthy experience, women being regarded as more supportive, more cooperative, more patient and less competitive than men. Such groups were more likely to take time to stop
30 and notice things around them, and to share the enjoyable experience of riding deep into the countryside, rather than to feel the need to ride for riding's sake or to become competitive. Men were considered to be too
35 keen on taking risks, and showing off the strong points of their bicycles. However, some women felt that mixed company encouraged them to try harder.

Buying the right bike can be a tricky task.
40 For most of the women, the first bike was either too large (most common) or too small: good advice seemed hard to come by. It is easy to get talked into buying a cheap and cheerful machine (or even a very expensive
45 one) by a shop assistant who doesn't see mountain biking from your point of view. Often, shop assistants don't consider that a not particularly strong woman might benefit more from a lighter bike than one built to
50 take rough treatment from a professional rider. Unhelpful shops seemed to come high on women's list of complaints. They were either too eager to sell products the buyer didn't want or need, or came out with
55 insulting comments. Some women didn't feel they were treated as legitimate customers. 'Is the bike for your son?' is not a helpful opener to someone prepared to fork out a large sum on a purchase for herself.
60 As for the riding itself, suggestions included starting with someone of your own level or a bit better, but not someone competitive, so as to gain experience and confidence gradually. Plan to cover fewer miles than you would
65 riding on a hard surface, and remember that there are few eating and watering places off-road. One reader was particularly encouraging: 'Once you start, you'll probably want to do more and discover a whole new
70 freedom – and that's precious.'

7   What do the words 'this end' (line 6) refer to?

    A   Having mountain bikes.
    B   Riding off-road.
    C   The gain in popularity.
    D   A means.

8   Why do many women take up mountain bikes?

    A   They want to spend more time with their husbands or friends.
    B   They are interested in cycling with women's groups.
    C   They are trying to prove that they are as capable as men.
    D   They want to get to areas which are difficult to reach otherwise.

9   What are the advantages of cycling in a women's group?

    A   The women do not have to try so hard.
    B   It is easier to compete with other women.
    C   The group atmosphere is more pleasant.
    D   Everyone has similar bicycles.

10   The writer says that shop assistants often

    A   have a tendency to talk too much.
    B   do not understand what women really need.
    C   are not interested in selling bikes to women.
    D   do not know enough about mountain bikes.

11   The words 'fork out' in line 58 mean

    A   spend.
    B   take.
    C   have.
    D   earn.

12   What advice does the text give to women who begin riding mountain bikes?

    A   They should ride as much as they can.
    B   They shouldn't forget to stop and eat.
    C   They shouldn't push themselves too hard at first.
    D   They should ride to experience more freedom.

13   Where does the text come from?

    A   An article in a cycling magazine.
    B   A brochure encouraging women to cycle.
    C   An advertisement for mountain bicycles.
    D   A report on the advantages of cycling.

PART 3

You are going to read a newspaper article in which a TV presenter describes how she got her job. Eight sentences have been removed from the article. Choose from the sentences **A–I** the one which fits each gap (**14–20**). There is one extra sentence which you do not need to use. There is an example at the beginning (**0**).

Mark your answers **on the separate answer sheet**.

Jilly Halliday: Sky TV Presenter

When I was a kid, I always wanted a career in entertainment, but I don't think I would ever have imagined becoming a television producer! **0** **I** I took a number of exams, including those for the Royal Academy of Dancing. I also won quite a few trophies and medals.

The hard work obviously paid off because at the age of 15 I was offered a contract with the world-famous dance group *The Bluebell Girls*. **14** My career decision hit the headlines as I turned down the offer, and I decided to stay on at school and get my O-levels.

After passing my exams, I knew I would need an Equity card in order to work on stage. Equity is an actors' union that provides services to entertainers: being a member tells the world that you are a professional. To become a member you have to prove that you have gained relevant experience. **15** Finally my dream of appearing in a West End musical became a reality as I was offered a role in the chorus of *42nd Street*.

In order to extend my training I studied for a degree in performing and contemporary arts and also did a course at the Actors' Institute. The degree course was very theoretical; the Actors' Institute course was more practical. **16** There are a number of drama courses available and it is worth making sure that you spend time researching what is on offer.

Getting good training was definitely worth while as it helped prepare me for auditions and built my confidence. **17** This eventually led to my first presenting job – a promotional film for a glass factory!

Things have certainly looked up since then. I now work for Sky TV. I present 16 hours of live television a week which includes everything from live cookery demonstrations to DIY. **18** I still do promotional films for large companies and also do commercials from time to time.

Although my job may sound glamorous, it is very hard work and it's certainly not a job for people who need a routine. There is no such thing as a typical day as a presenter. If I'm on the breakfast slot, I'm usually up at around 4 a.m.; if I'm launching the midnight hour, I'm not home until 3 a.m. **19** I wouldn't change it for the world.

I must say that I think it's a great job and I still get a thrill from going to work! **20** You also have to be flexible and adaptable and willing to do just about anything to gain experience. My advice for anyone wanting a career in the media is to stay focused and take advantage of every opportunity that you can – it's good experience and you never know what it might lead to.

A Although it was a great opportunity, I really felt that it was important to get some academic qualifications and concentrate on my real ambition – getting a part in a West End musical.

B I also get to interview famous guests such as Paul McKenna and Tony Blackburn.

C I don't think that there is a typical way into television, and if there is, I don't think that I've taken it.

D I got mine by working as a dancer in Blackpool for a summer season.

E It covered areas such as voice training, methods of acting and performance.

F It's the price you pay to do this type of work and you have to go into it with your eyes open.

G Once I'd finished training, I spent two years working for a number of small theatre companies and began doing voice-overs for videos and television.

H I think that a successful television career requires a combination of enthusiasm, determination and hard work.

I I began dancing school at the age of two, studying ballet, tap and jazz.

PART 4

You are going to read a magazine article in which a number of students express their opinions about school uniforms. Some of them are in secondary school, and some of them are in sixth form college, where students in Britain can go after secondary school.

For questions **22–35**, decide in which of the sections of the article (**A–F**) this opinion is expressed. Some of the sections may be chosen more than once. When more than one answer is required, these may be given in any order. There is an example at the beginning (**0**).

Mark your answers **on the separate answer sheet**.

In which section do the following opinions or facts appear?

Boys and girls should be treated equally as far as their appearance is concerned.	**0** F		
It can be good to be told what to wear.	**21**	**22**	**23**
Not having a uniform can cause students to feel bad.	**24**	**25**	
Not having a uniform means spending more money.	**26**	**27**	
Wearing a uniform prevents you from developing your character.	**28**		
What you wear doesn't really matter.	**29**		
What you wear in school prepares you for dressing later in life.	**30**		
It would be better if the actual uniforms were different.	**31**		
In some schools, students have had problems with the administration over appearance.	**32**		
A school uniform means you have to develop your own personality.	**33**		
Wearing a uniform helps to build a school identity.	**34**		
It is good to wear different clothes out of school.	**35**		

Do you think school uniforms are an old-fashioned way of suppressing a pupil's identity or a sensible method of stopping youngsters from turning the classroom into a fashion parade? David Lloyd enquires ...

A

Jenny Keating and Vicky O'Gorman attend Birkenhead Sixth Form College where no uniform is required.

Vicky O'Gorman: 'I didn't like wearing uniforms in secondary school, but it was better than getting your normal clothes dirty. In the sixth form you feel like you have to spend more time on clothes to look OK whereas in school there was nothing to worry about. You just threw on your uniform every day, which was nice.'

Vicky believes that, for many students, there is an added financial burden of having to keep up with the latest fashions. 'In our college most people just wear what they feel comfortable in. But there's always a certain group who get to the new fashions and expensive labels first and expect everyone else to follow them. And this often leads to jealousy or resentment. It gets on my nerves sometimes having to wear the same clothes at the weekend that I do during the week, especially if they're all in the wash!'

B

Jenny Keating: 'I don't think sixth-formers should wear uniforms. Once you get to sixth form college everyone is stronger as an individual and trying to express their individuality. If they've got a uniform on, it could harm their development.'

As the saying goes, Jenny doesn't believe that you should judge a book by its cover. 'I don't think it's important for us to look smart, we're here to study. Just because you wear a uniform, this doesn't make you more responsible,' she said.

C

Students at Calday Grange Grammar School for Boys have to wear the school uniform and tie – and those staying on into the sixth form must replace it with a similar, smart jacket and tie: 'As one would be expected to wear in business,' explains a teacher.

D

Edward Clarke and Tim Roberts have just sat their exams and are moving up to the sixth form in September.

Edward Clarke: 'I think it can be cruel for some pupils when school has a non-uniform day because they feel terrible if they can't afford decent clothes. A school uniform enforces discipline and gives the students a sense of belonging.' Agreeing with the school sixth form's 'jacket and tie' policy, Edward adds: 'I'll be wearing a sports jacket for the sixth form. I think it's a good idea to have greater choice, but it's important to have guidelines, otherwise too much emphasis would be placed on what to wear.'

E

Tim Roberts: 'I'd rather be wearing a uniform than casual clothes, it saves my Mum a lot of cash.' Tim believes that wearing designer labels does not make you more of an 'individual'. 'If anything, a school uniform encourages you to develop your own character more. Because you all have to wear the same clothes, you have to try harder to make your individual character stand out. The one problem with uniform is that it's not very practical to wear all day. It's also very uncomfortable in the summer – the blazers are very heavy.'

F

• Six Essex boys won a fight to keep their hair on! The headmaster wanted the boys to get their hair cut. The school found out that it could be breaking the Sex Discrimination Act unless it ordered all the girls to shorten their hair as well.

• In Nottingham, pupils at one sweltering school organised a protest over a ban on shorts. It was summer, and the poor boys' legs were getting overheated – so was the headmaster, who suspended them all!

Paper 2 – Writing

PART 1

You **must** answer this question.

1 You have bought a vacuum cleaner by mail order from a firm in Great Britain and you have found out that it does not fit its description. Look at the advertisement with the comments which you have written on it and write a letter to the company you bought the vacuum cleaner from, asking for appropriate action on their part.

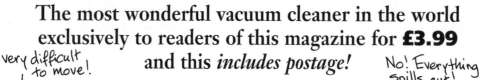

The most wonderful vacuum cleaner in the world exclusively to readers of this magazine for **£3.99** and this *includes postage!*

very difficult to move!

No! Everything spills out!

For years you have been wondering how to keep both your carpets and your floors clean, looking for a vacuum cleaner that would pick up everything . . . be mobile . . . clean stairs . . . clean under furniture . . . be easily handled.

THE ANSWER: our new *whizz-vac*.
The vacuum cleaner that is a **wizard in disguise!**

As a mail order company we are able to offer this price, which is lower than at any store. We are also the only company from whom you can order by mail FROM ABROAD!

Not true - many shops sell it cheaper!

So order now from: Conman appliances, Unit 55, Whitley Wood Estate, Berkshire, or order by phone: Tel: 02734 959595

never any answer!

furniture damaged after 2 uses

Write a **letter of between 120 and 180 words** in an appropriate style. Do not write any addresses.

PART 2

Write an answer to **one** of the questions **2–5** in this part. Write your answer in **120–180** words in an appropriate style.

2   A publishing house is putting together a guide for visitors to your country. You have been asked to write a short article describing the weather in the different seasons and different areas in your country, and the types of clothes that visitors should bring with them for each season and area.

Write your **article**.

3   You have decided to enter a competition in response to the advertisement below:

YOUR CHANCE TO BUILD THE HOUSE OF YOUR DREAMS!

DESCRIBE THE HOUSE OF YOUR DREAMS, AND YOU MAY
WIN UP TO HALF THE COST OF BUILDING IT.

Write your **composition** for the competition

4   The Education authorities in your town would like to improve the state of libraries in the town. You have been asked to submit a report about the libraries in your area, and suggest possible improvements to the library service.

Write your **report**.

5   **Background reading texts**

Answer **one** of the following two questions based on your reading of **one** of the set books.

(a) Did the book help you understand anything about yourself, your own country or current events in the world? Write a short **composition** explaining in what way the text you read did this.

(b) Write a **letter** to a pen-friend in an English speaking country, discussing the book you read and explaining why you recommend (or do not recommend) this book to her/him. Do not write any addresses.

Paper 3 – Use of English

PART 1

For questions **1-15**, read the text below and decide which word **A, B, C** or **D** best fits each space.
There is an example at the beginning (**0**).
Mark your answers **on the separate answer sheet**.

Example:

0   **A**   others   **B**   other   **C**   one other   **D**   another

0	A	B	C	D
	▬▬	▭	▭	▭

The four-minute mile

It is the nature of athletic records that they are broken and their place is taken by (**0**)..... . Yet in many sports (**1**)..... , there is a mark which is not (**2**)..... in itself, but which becomes a legend as athletes (**3**)..... to break it. The most (**4**)..... of these is the attempt to run the mile in (**5**)..... than four minutes.

In 1945, the mile record was (**6**)..... to 4 minutes, 1.5 seconds. And there, for nine years, it stuck. Then, in 1954, a medical student (**7**)..... Roger Bannister decided to try and break the record. He had been (**8**)..... for this day since running the mile in 4 minutes, 2 seconds the (**9**)..... year.

Two other runners set the pace for him, and (**10**)..... 250 yards to go he burst ahead for the finish. He wrote (**11**)..... : 'My body had exhausted all its energy, but it (**12**)..... on running just the same ... Those (**13**)..... few seconds seemed never-ending. I could see the line of the finishing tape ... I jumped like a man making a desperate attempt to save himself from danger ...'

Bannister's time was 3 minutes, 59.4 seconds. (**14**)..... this record has been broken on many (**15**)..... since, Bannister's achievement will never be forgotten.

1	A	happenings	B	events	C	games	D	matches
2	A	central	B	major	C	significant	D	considerable
3	A	try	B	try on	C	try out	D	try for
4	A	known	B	public	C	noticeable	D	famous
5	A	smaller	B	less	C	lower	D	under
6	A	broken down	B	lessened	C	decreased	D	brought down
7	A	entitled	B	called	C	nicknamed	D	known
8	A	trying	B	studying	C	running	D	training

9	A	early	B	previous	C	past	D	former
10	A	on	B	in	C	with	D	by
11	A	afterwards	B	then	C	next	D	after
12	A	went	B	continued	C	ran	D	got
13	A	last	B	late	C	latest	D	later
14	A	But	B	In spite of	C	However	D	Although
15	A	times	B	times	C	occasions	D	incidents

PART 2

For questions **16–30**, read the text below and think of the word which best fits each space. Use only one word in each space. There is an example at the beginning (**0**). Write your word **on the separate answer sheet**.

Example:

0	*its*	0

How television was invented

Television owes **(0)**.............. origins to many inventors. But it was the single-minded determination of an amateur inventor, John Logie Baird, that led **(16)**.............. the first live television broadcast.

Born in Scotland in 1888 and educated in Glasgow, John Logie Baird earned a living **(17)**.............. a razor-blade salesman. In the 1890s Guglielmo Marconi showed that sound could **(18)**................ sent by radio waves. Baird became convinced that a similar system could transmit a picture. He spent most of **(19)**.............. spare time working on his ideas in his tiny workshop without **(20)**.............. commercial support. He **(21)**.............. to use his **(22)**.............. earnings to continue his research.

In 1924, Baird successfully transmitted the general outline of a figure over more **(23)**.............. 3 metres. He continued to experiment and **(24)**.............. October 25, 1925 transmitted a recognisable image of a doll. He ran **(25)**.............. to the office on the ground floor and persuaded one of the office boys to come upstairs. **(26)**.............. boy became the first living image transmitted by television. Overnight, Baird became famous and the money **(27)**.............. he needed to continue his research was at **(28)**.............. made available. In 1927 he made a transmission from London to Glasgow and in 1928 he made **(29)**.............. from London to New York. He continued experimenting **(30)**.............. spent his last years exploring the possibility of colour television.

59

PART 3

For questions **31–40**, complete the second sentence so that is has a similar meaning to the first sentence, using the word given. **Do not change the word given**. You must use between two and five words, including the word given. There is an example at the beginning (**0**).
Write only the missing words **on the separate answer sheets**.

Example:

0 Could you please go to desk No. 15?
way
Could you please .... to desk No. 15?

The gap can be filled by the words 'make your way', so you write:

0	make your way

31 Don't you regret not learning to swim?
wish
Don't you .... swim?

32 Working outdoors is much nicer than working in an office.
nice
Working in an office is not .... outdoors.

33 Maria will be ready any minute, and then we must leave.
soon
We must leave .... ready.

34 The last time I saw him was when I lived in London.
since
I .... I lived in London.

35 Why don't you telephone me later to discuss this?
give
Why don't you .... later to discuss this?

36 I was on the point of leaving the office.
about
I was just .... office.

37 I am fed up with his behaviour.
enough
I .... his behaviour.

38 Our senior manager is dealing with this matter, sir.
being
The matter .... our senior manager, sir.

39 I don't mind whether we have the meeting today or tomorrow.
makes
It .... me whether we have the meeting today or tomorrow.

40 I've got to get a new computer.
need
What I really .... new computer.

PART 4

For questions **41–55,** read the text below and look carefully at each line. Some of the lines are correct, and some have a word which should not be there.
If a line is correct, put a tick (✓) by the number **on the separate answer sheet.** If a line has a word which should **not** be there, write the word **on the separate answer sheet.** There are two examples at the beginning (**0** and **00**).

Examples:

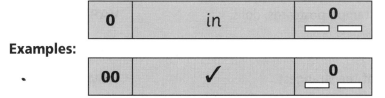

Exchange programmes

0   In nowadays it is becoming increasingly popular for

00 students to go on an exchange programme. This is

41 especially popular in the Europe. In such programmes,

42 students can to go abroad and study at a foreign university

43 for a term or two, and these studies count towards their

44 degree. This arrangement has several of advantages.

45 Students have the opportunity to be practise the foreign

46 languages what they have learnt in school. They meet

47 different cultures and experience a different way of life. In

48 addition, they learn about different ways of thinking in their

49 own studying subject and get a broader view of the issues.

50 For example, one Austrian student who was studying at

51 agriculture found different types of the farming in England

52 very interesting. Finally, they also meet to exchange

53 students from other countries, so they experience a really

54 international environment. This experience will hopefully

55 result in a more better understanding between nations.

PART 5

For questions **56–65**, read the text below. Use the word given in capitals at the end of each line to form a word that fits in the space in the same line. There is an example at the beginning (**0**).
Write your word **on the separate answer sheet**.

Example:

0	*variety*	**0** ▭ ▭

Collecting eggcups

People collect a large **(0)**............... of objects: stamps, postcards, dolls.	**VARY**
Some people collect objects which are connected with **(56)**...............	**HISTORY**
events or with **(57)**............... people. But one of the strangest	**FAME**
(58)............... is that of eggcups. Kevin Murphy of Bradford in	**COLLECT**
Yorkshire has 10,000 of them. Not **(59)**............... , his favourite eggcup	**SURPRISE**
is one in the shape of a **(60)**............... Yorkshireman. Kevin's hobby	**TYPE**
began seven years ago, after he **(61)**............... an elephant eggcup to a	**LOAN**
granddaughter who took such a **(62)**............... to it she insisted on keeping it.	**LIKE**
Kevin saw a few eggcups he liked at a **(63)**............... at a local shop,	**SELL**
and started collecting them.	
Others like Kevin's eggcups too. 'I have just bought a **(64)**...............	**REPLACE**
for one of my favourites, which **(65)**............... disappeared last week,'	**MYSTERY**
he said.	

Paper 4 – Listening

PART 1

You will hear people talking in eight different situations. For questions **1–8**, choose the best answer, **A**, **B** or **C**.

1   Listen to these two people talking about music. What do we learn about the woman?
   A She plays with an amateur group.
   B She is a professional musician.
   C She only goes to concerts as a listener.

| 1 |

2   Listen to a man talking about a football match. Who is the person speaking?
   A A sports announcer.
   B A team supporter.
   C A sportsman.

| 2 |

3   You are sitting on a bus when you hear two people talking. Where have the two speakers been?
   A To a concert.
   B To a play.
   C To a film.

| 3 |

4   Listen to this man talking on the telephone. What is the man describing?
   A A washing machine.
   B A fridge.
   C A dishwasher.

| 4 |

5   Listen to this conversation about a private lesson. Who are the speakers?
   A A student and a teacher.
   B A secretary and a teacher.
   C A secretary and a student.

| 5 |

6   Listen to this conversation about the performance of a play. What does the man think about the performance?
   A It was funny.
   B It was bad.
   C It was good.

| 6 |

7   Listen to a teacher speaking about different courses. Which course does she think the student should take?
   A The preparatory course.
   B A language course.
   C An evening course.

| 7 |

8   Listen to this excerpt from a radio programme. What is the programme devoted to?
   A Geography.
   B Health.
   C Food.

| 8 |

63

PART 2

You will hear a talk about the history of fingerprints.
For questions **9–18**, complete the notes which summarise what the speaker says. You will need to write a word or a short phrase in each box.

The Measurement Method was not an effective way of	**9**
but it helped the police to	**10**
It was a kind of	**11**
Fingerprinting was first invented by	**12**
in	**13**
In the South American system there were	**14**
The South American experts were the first to use fingerprints to	**15**
Nowadays, identification is carried out first by	**16**
and then by	**17**
It is possible to take fingerprints even when the criminals	**18**

PART 3

You will hear five different people talking about holidays they had.
For questions **19–23**, choose from the list **A–F** which kind of holiday each
person had. Use the letters only once. There is one extra letter which you do
not need to use.

A   a week on the beach

B   a cycling holiday

C   mountain climbing

D   a walking tour

E   a camping holiday

F   a boating holiday

Speaker 1	19
Speaker 2	20
Speaker 3	21
Speaker 4	22
Speaker 5	23

PART 4

You will hear a conversation between three people who are going for a meal together.
Answer questions **24–30**, by writing   **B**   (for Bridget)
                                          M   (for Maria)
                                    or   **D**   (for Daniel).

24 Who cannot make up their mind?	24
25 Who gets annoyed?	25
26 Who makes a decision?	26
27 Who has already been to Michel's?	27
28 Who is vegetarian?	28
29 Who is very busy?	29
30 Who makes a strong objection?	30

65

Paper 5 – Speaking

The photos and pictures the interlocutor refers to appear on pages 120–122.

PART 1

The interlocutor encourages each of the candidates in turn to give personal information about themselves by asking questions such as:

Where are you from?
How long have you lived here/there?
What is it like living here/there?
How do you usually spend your free time?
What are your plans for the future?

PART 2

The interlocutor gives each of the candidates in turn two photographs to look at and gives the following instructions:

Candidate A, here are your two pictures. Please let Candidate B see them. They show two different sports. Candidate A, I'd like you to compare and contrast these pictures saying how you feel about sports like these. When Candidate A has finished, I'd like you, Candidate B, to tell us which sport you would choose if you were offered a free course for one of them.

* * *

Candidate B, here are your two pictures. Please let Candidate A see them. They show two different shopping situations. Candidate B, I'd like you to compare and contrast these pictures saying how you feel about places like these. When Candidate B has finished, I'd like you, Candidate A, to tell us which of the two places you would go to for your shopping.

PART 3

The interlocutor gives the candidates some pictures to look at and gives the following instructions:

You are in charge of a class party given for one of your classmates' birthday. The party is taking place in a large room which you have to set up for the event. Look at the plan of the room and decide how you would arrange it for the different activities and where you would put the different things shown in the pictures.

PART 4

The interlocutor encourages the candidates to develop the topic raised in Part 3 by asking questions such as:

Do young people go to many parties in your country?
Do people play party games in your country?
Do people have large birthday parties in your country?
What events do people celebrate with a large party?
What types of dances would people dance at parties that you go to?
What types of music would people play at parties that you go to?

Practice exam 4

Paper 1 – Reading

PART 1

You are going to read a newspaper article about flying kites. Choose the
most suitable heading from the list **A–I** for each part (**1–7**) of the article.
There is one extra heading which you do not need to use. There is an
example at the beginning (**0**).
Mark your answers **on the separate answer sheet**.

A	The future: newer, better, more expensive.
B	Everything about kite-flying has changed.
C	All shapes and sizes.
D	Even you can afford it.
E	Achieving official recognition.
F	The excitement of the future.
G	The principle of the new designs.
H	Old designs from new materials.
I	The sky does have a limit.

WILLIAM GREEN discovers a new look for a long-popular sport

0 | I

On the wall of Martin Lester's kite workshop are the following words:

> 'No bird flies too high
> If he flies with his own wings.'

Not everyone agrees. If you feel like breaking the world kite altitude record of 12,471 feet, you will have to obtain a special permit. Otherwise, the legal limit set for kite flying is a mere 180 feet.

1

Lester, one of a dozen or so designers in this country who actually make a living out of kites, says the sport is no longer a matter of 'kids running up and down a beach, with large wet bits of paper behind them.' New materials, new flying techniques and fresh ideas have turned the subject inside out.

2

The traditional British kite was made of pieces of thin cotton cloth stretched on a frame of wood. The revolution in kite technology began in the mid-1970s with the introduction of lighter materials. The new light kites needed wind speeds of as little as 5 miles per hour to fly in, so kite flyers could fly their creations more successfully and more often. More daring and more colourful kites – still using past designs – began to appear.

3

In the old days, to get the kite in the air and hold it steady in a stiff wind was considered enough fun. As this became easier, designers turned to a more exciting possibility – the steerable kite. The new designs are steered by means of twin lines which are held one in each hand. Twin-lined kites are designed to be unstable, and once in the air they never keep still. The idea is to pull at one or other line to make the kite fly up, down and sideways, or in circles and loops. The basic skills of working such kites are easily learned, but mastering the art is an athletic occupation.

4

In twin-line kite competitions complex patterns are drawn in the sky and judged for speed and accuracy. Such figure competitions, aerial ballets and aerobatic displays have become extremely popular, and as a result a number of semi-professional kite teams have been formed. There is even talk of making kite flying an Olympic sport.

5

Some kite flyers go for huge kites with many hundreds of square feet of sail, so big that they have to be licensed as aeroplanes. Large 'lifting' kites are often used to carry cameras for taking photographs from the air. At the other end of the scale, tiny kites may be no larger than postage stamps.

6

Even with the best new materials and all the modern additions, it is still very hard to spend more than a couple of hundred pounds on a kite. Lester's most expensive kite is £120. You only pay more if you want a hand-made kite, a huge box construction, or else a collector's Japanese kite, made of painted *washi* paper and special bamboo. Such kites look beautiful but nobody would dare to fly them, as they can be destroyed by a single crash landing, or the lightest shower of rain.

7

The next development is likely to be the four-string kite, which is said to be twice as much fun. Developed in the US, there are only half-a-dozen such kites in this country at present. Lester has already tried one. 'It took me four hours,' he says happily, 'to get any sense of being in control.'

PART 2

You are going to read a text about taking a year off from studying before going on to university. For questions **8–14**, choose the answer (**A, B, C** or **D**) which you think fits best according to the text.
Mark your answers **on the separate answer sheet**.

Unfortunately, many students overlook the value of taking a year off from their studies. Far from being a year wasted, a gap year between school and university could actually be of benefit to your
5 future, especially if you make the most of it by working and travelling abroad. Not only are you likely to increase your self-confidence by living in another country, you'll add valuable work experience to your CV – a bonus when it comes to
10 job hunting after college.

Planning to take 12 to 15 months off need not be difficult if you do your homework. Although travelling or working abroad for voluntary organisations may prove expensive if you lack
15 sufficient funds, it is possible to combine your travels with paid work experience.

Since 1962, BUNAC, a non-profit organisation, has enabled thousands of full-time students to work in America, Canada and Australia each year.
20 There is a wide range of programmes to choose from and they are designed to be self-financing, so you should be able to earn back your initial expenses and have sufficient money to pay for your post-work travels.

25 Work America and Work Canada are open to full time students and those who have postponed their entry and have a place at a university for the following year. Those taking part in the programme can take almost any job
30 anywhere for the summer (up to 12 months in Canada). It is even possible to pack fish in Alaska, if that appeals! Most, however, would tend to work in temporary jobs within the tourism industry, mainly in restaurants and
35 hotels.

BUNACAMP Counsellors places both students and non-students at children's summer camps in the USA. Those aged between 19 and 35, with relevant experience of working with groups of
40 children, can spend up to eight weeks teaching sporting, arts and dramatic activities at camp

and have time to travel around North America afterwards. For those who would rather work behind the scenes, the KAMP programme places
45 students in kitchen and maintenance positions. Both programmes include return transatlantic flights, free board and lodging and pocket-money.

Work Australia offers 18–25 year olds with
50 more time to spare, the opportunity to work and travel 'down under' for up to 12 months. There are several departures from London or Los Angeles throughout August, September and October so it's an ideal programme for gap-year
55 students or those who have just graduated. You can even link it to one of the North American programmes to get the most out of the experience.

Kathryn Jackson spent a year travelling
60 around Australia. 'My most enjoyable job in Australia was as a receptionist, cook and cleaner at "Backpack Australia", a crazy place in Adelaide,' said Kathryn. 'I left there with great memories and a bursting address book.'

65 Over the next month Kathryn travelled around in a station wagon with friends. 'We went diving at the Great Barrier Reef, drove through sugarcane fields and tropical fruit plantations, watched the sunset over Ayers Rock
70 and lived on cheese and jam sandwiches. It was incredible!' On the importance of her year off, Kathryn said, 'I feel my trip has taught me a lot – from the importance of tolerance and experiencing new cultures to how to cook. My
75 self-confidence has improved amazingly.'

Taking a year off does require forward planning, so you'll need to apply this October for next year's summer programme. BUNAC arranges visas, flights, airport greetings and
80 back-up support for participants, which makes organising your trip very easy. All you have to do is decide where you want to go!

8 The main advantage of a year out is that you can

   A   finance your studies.
   B   have a good time.
   C   gain experience.
   D   relax before university.

9 'if you do your homework' (line 12) means

   A   if you manage to get good grades.
   B   if you make the right enquiries.
   C   if you are a hard-working student.
   D   if you work well during your year out.

10 According to the text, taking time off between school and university is

   A   quite difficult to arrange.
   B   an extremely uncommon thing.
   C   impossible if you have no money.
   D   better if you go abroad.

11 The word 'Most' (line 32) refers to

   A   the tourism industry.
   B   full-time students.
   C   those taking part in the programme.
   D   temporary jobs.

12 To work with BUNACAMP Counsellors you have to

   A   be a student in full-time education.
   B   have worked with children before.
   C   be willing to travel around North America.
   D   be willing to pay for your flight.

13 What does Kathryn Jackson say about her year in Australia?

   A   It was a rewarding experience.
   B   The work was very easy.
   C   She didn't like the food.
   D   She made one or two new friends.

14 Where does this text come from?

   A   A student magazine.
   B   A tourism brochure.
   C   A university leaflet.
   D   An airline advertisement.

PART 3

You are going to read a newspaper article about a day in the life of an actor. Eight sentences have been removed from the article. Choose from the sentences **A–I** the one which fits each gap (**15–21**). There is one extra sentence which you do not need to use. There is an example at the beginning (**0**).
Mark your answers **on the separate answer sheet**.

A I do take pride in what I wear, but I was really surprised to be listed among the ten best-dressed men in the country, recently.

B I was on stage for four hours every night, and I found that the fitter I felt physically, the better my performance was.

C I tend to read about three pages, then I fall asleep.

D I'd love to do more musical theatre.

E But I like adventure and I enjoyed taking off for Africa and Australia with only a backpack.

F My grandfather deals with my fan mail because I haven't got the time to do it all.

G I have a very disciplined attitude to most things.

H There's one little girl who writes to me every couple of weeks.

I I also enjoy running or playing football in one of the big London parks.

My kind of day

WHAT TIME I get up depends on what I've been doing the night before. I usually have a bowl of cereal with cold milk – the noise it makes helps wake me up. When I'm not working, I spend a lot of time at health clubs, gyms and dance studios. There are five or six I go to regularly; each one provides different facilities, like weights and stamina training. **0** **I**

You need strength and stamina to be an actor. A few years ago I played Heathcliff in a stage version of *Wuthering Heights*. **15**
I was at drama school with Daniel Day Lewis – we still go running together sometimes – and he believes, like I do, that a lean body means a healthy mind. Otherwise, how would he have given such a brilliant performance in *My Left Foot*?

I go to the theatre and the cinema about three times a week. I'm into musicals, and I train with a voice coach. **16** I did a Noel Coward concert last year, so I spent weeks beforehand listening to his music on tapes.

When we were making the first television series of *Bread* four years ago, the producer warned us that we would probably all become famous, so it wasn't unexpected. Now it's just part of my life. It's only boring when you're really tired and you've had a late night. I don't like people being rude, but I'm happy to sign autographs if they ask me nicely. **17** I send it all to him in Manchester, where I come from, and then I go up every other weekend just to go through it with him.

18 She never asks for anything, though. I think it's just that she likes keeping in touch and I always enjoy reading her letters.

I usually buy two newspapers, one tabloid and a quality paper. I like reading the sports pages and travel articles. My bedtime reading is normally a book by Laurens van der Post. **19**

If I'm really busy, with a photo session and a rehearsal and a recording all in the same day, the hardest thing is making sure I've got a shirt ironed. When you're a busy bachelor, you haven't always got time to have things washed and ironed, so you end up having six pairs of everything. **20** It's amazing to think there are people out there who care so much about what you wear. I like Continental clothes, American sports clothes and the traditional English blazer look.

Food's a chore, I'm afraid. I don't live to eat: I eat to live. I can just make myself a plate of pasta but if I'm seeing friends, we eat out. I'm so busy now I don't have time for holidays, and I've never been one for lying on the beach. **21**

At the moment I've got everything and, unlike Adrian in *Bread*, I'm having the most wonderful time anybody could wish for.

PART 4

You are going to read a magazine article in which a number of people describe their eating habits. For questions **22–35** choose from the list of people (**A–G**) in the box. Some of the people may be chosen more than once. When more than one answer is required, these may be given in any order. There is an example at the beginning (**0**).
Mark your answers **on the separate answer sheet**.

A	the Norris family	**D**	Caroline Scott	**F**	Ade Bakare
B	Michael Norris	**E**	the Mughal family	**G**	Ade Bakare's mother
C	the Scott family				

Which of the families or people:

eats together every morning?	**0** C	
almost never eats together?	**22**	
feel that eating together keeps the family close?	**23**	**24**
cook food that is healthy?	**25**	**26**
eats a lot of frozen food?	**27**	
spends a long time cooking?	**28**	
cooks in a large group?	**29**	
often does not eat at home?	**30**	
thinks children should be taught table manners?	**31**	
don't have fixed eating habits?	**32**	**33**
have special meals at the weekend?	**34**	**35**

For some people it's dinner. Others call it supper.
Whatever you know it as, the evening meal is not what it was.
Paul Richardson **finds out who eats what and when.**

Separate tables

The Norris family is a monument to modern frozen-food technology. 'I can't remember the last time we all ate together,' says husband Michael Norris. 'Mostly the food comes out of the freezer and goes straight into the microwave. We have two dining-tables but they never get used, not unless my mother-in-law, who lives with us, cooks something.' The children, Sophie and Ben, eat when they come home from school, while watching TV. Pat Norris, who works irregular hours and travels a lot, boils soup and makes a salad when she's at home; Michael often eats out. It's informal, but everyone likes it.

The art of course eating

The Scott family like a bit of formality in their lives. 'We're not stuffy,' insists Caroline, 'but we always have napkins and white linen and flowers on the table. My husband always has a bath before dinner, and we always change clothes. I think it's important for the children to have good manners.' Caroline drives across town to find food that's not 'full of all sorts of nasty chemicals'. The result is meals that 'sometimes take an hour and a half, at least, and longer at weekends.' The children attend an equally civilised breakfast served at 8.00 a.m. prompt in the dining-room. 'It's a sort of ritual so we can all see one another. We all feel it's important,' says Caroline, who doesn't have a microwave and does most of the cooking herself. 'I seem to spend a lot of time cooking,' she says. 'I don't know why. I suppose it's because we've always done it.'

Spice of life

The evening meal at the Mughal household brings together three generations: 18-month-old Sameer, his sister Nina, three, parents Rubina and Haleem and the grandparents. Sometimes there are other family members as well. 'People catch up with each other at meal times,' says cousin Shamreen. 'We usually eat quite late, about 8.30 or 9.00 p.m., because we wait for everyone to get in. It's important to have a table that's laid out, although during the week it's usually just a couple of dishes. Weekends are a bit more special!' Rubina will normally cook a rice dish, a meat curry and sometimes a salad. Quite a lot for one pair of hands, but there are always people around to help – and, as Shamreen points out, a lot of Asian dishes can be made the night before, or even frozen.

Student life

Ade Bakare, 23 years old and a student at Thames Polytechnic, tends towards the irregular in his dining habits. Between 9.00 p.m. and 11.00 p.m. about three times a week, 'depending on how we're feeling', Ade and his flatmates settle down to a meal. The menu may vary between Kentucky Fried Chicken and 'ebba', an African dish made of ground rice. 'Obviously fast food is easier, and none of the other guys are very good cooks,' says Ade. The taste for African cooking comes from his mother's house, where the set-up is rather different. 'I'd always sit down at the table with my mother. The food is much more substantial, much more nutritious, partly because she wants to ensure that I am eating properly.'

Paper 2 – Writing

PART 1

You **must** answer this question.

1   You have seen the advertisement below, and are writing on behalf of a friend to find out more information about the competition. Your friend plays a traditional musical instrument, and is going to Britain for a few months. Using this information, the advertisement, and the notes which you and your friend have made, write a letter asking for the information you need.

Could you be this year's
South West Young Musician
Only British?
Other nationalities? **of the Year?**   What kind of music? All kinds?

South West Television is seeking applications from young performers and composers. There will also be a variety of workshops for small groups. Age? Not clear?

So if you're a performer aged 19 and under, or a composer aged 24 and under, Britain's most famous television programme for young musical talent would like to hear from you.

Entry forms and further details available from:
Room E214
South Tower
South West Television Centre
Highfield Road
Bristol

Write a **letter** of between **120 and 180** words in an appropriate style. Do not write any addresses.

PART 2

Write an answer to **one** of the questions **2–5** in this part. Write your answer in **120–180** words in an appropriate style.

2   Your town council has suggested that a large park near your home should be sold and a housing estate built there. Write a letter to the town council supporting or opposing this suggestion.

Write your **letter**. Do not write any addresses.

3   You have decided to enter a short story competition. The competition rules say that the title of the story must be: 'The Longest Journey'.

Write your **story** for the competition.

4   Your teacher has asked you to choose one of your hobbies and write a composition describing it and explaining why you find it worthwhile.

Write your **composition**.

5   **Background reading texts**

Answer **one** of the following two questions based on your reading of **one** of the set books.

(a)   The English Drama Club in your school is looking for a new play and is looking into the possibility of turning the book you have read into a play. Write a **report** discussing the suitability of this book for such a project.

(b)   You have seen the advertisement below in a newspaper and have decided to enter the competition advertised.

TRANSLATION TRAVEL AWARD

This could be your opportunity to win a short course in translation in Britain! Write a short composition explaining why a book you like should be translated into your first language. The ten best compositions will win a translation course!

Write your **composition**.

Paper 3 – Use of English

PART 1

For questions **1–15**, read the text below and decide which word **A**, **B**, **C** or **D** best fits each space. There is an example at the beginning (**0**). Mark your answers **on the separate answer sheet**.

Example:

0   **A** invented   **B** created   **C** originated   **D** started

0	A	B	C	D
	▬	▭	▭	▭

Traffic Lights

The first traffic signal was (**0**)..... by a railway signalling engineer. It was installed (**1**)..... the Houses of Parliament in 1868. It (**2**)..... like any railway signal of the time, and was operated by gas. (**3**)..... , it exploded and killed a policeman, and the accident (**4**)..... further development until cars became common.

(**5**)..... traffic lights are an American invention. Red-green (**6**)..... were installed in Cleveland in 1914. Three-colour signals, operated (**7**)..... hand from a tower in the (**8**)..... of the street, were installed in New York in 1918. The (**9**)..... lights of this type to (**10**)..... in Britain were in London, on the junction between St. James's Street and Piccadilly, in 1925. Automatic signals were installed (**11**)..... year later.

In the past, traffic lights were (**12**)..... . In New York, some lights had a statue on top. In Los Angeles the lights did not just (**13**)..... silently, but would ring bells to (**14**)..... the sleeping motorists of the 1930s. These are gone and have been (**15**)..... by standard models which are universally adopted.

1 A outside   B out   C out of   D outdoors

2 A resembled   B looked   C showed   D seemed

3 A However   B Therefore   C Although   D Despite

4 A forbade   B disappointed   C avoided   D discouraged

5 A New   B Recent   C Modern   D Late

6 A methods   B ways   C systems   D means

7 A by   B with   C through   D in

8 A middle   B heart   C focus   D halfway

9 A original   B primary   C first   D early

10 A show   B appear   C happen   D become

11 A a   B in the   C in a   D the

12 A various   B particular   C rare   D special

13 A change   B alter   C vary   D move

14 A rise   B raise   C wake   D get up

15 A reproduced   B replaced   C removed   D remained

PART 2

For questions **16–30**, read the text below and think of the word which best fits each space. Use only **one** word in each space. There is an example at the beginning **(0)**.
Write your word **on the separate answer sheet**.

Example: | **0** | *every* | **0** ▭ ▭ |

The great library in Alexandria

Today, there are libraries in almost **(0)**............... town in the world. Even in areas **(16)**............... there are no libraries, there are often mobile libraries which take books from one village to **(17)**............... . But in the days when books were copied by hand **(18)**............... than printed, libraries were very rare. The reason is simple: books took a very **(19)**............... time to produce, and there were far **(20)**............... copies of any given work around. The greatest library **(21)**............... all, that in Alexandria, had 54,000 books. In the ancient world, this number **(22)**............... considered huge. It was the first time that anyone **(23)**............... ever collected so many books from all around the world **(24)**............... one roof. There are many theories about **(25)**............... these books were lost. **(26)**............... is that the library accidentally burned down. Another is that one of the rulers of the city ordered the books to **(27)**............... burned. They were taken to various places and it took six months to burn them. **(28)**............... happened, the collection there was priceless. Many of the library's treasures were lost forever – some books were **(29)**............... recovered. We cannot even know **(30)**............... exactly the library contained.

PART 3

For questions **31–40**, complete the second sentence so that it has a similar meaning to the first sentence, using the word given. **Do not change the word given**. You must use between two and five words, including the word given. There is an example at the beginning. **(0)**
Write **only** the missing words **on the separate answer sheet**.

Example:

0   Your car really needs a wash.
     washed
     You really must .... soon.

The gap can be filled by the words 'get your car washed' or
'have your car washed', so you write:

| **0** | get your car washed | **or** | **0** | have your car washed |

31 People claim that he is the best tennis player of our times.
said
He .... best tennis player of our times.

32 They left early because they didn't want to get caught in the traffic.
avoid
They left early in order .... in the traffic.

33 Why didn't they tell me about these changes earlier?
should
I .... about these changes earlier.

34 Nobody plays this piece as beautifully as he does.
more
He plays this piece .... else.

35 If I don't leave now, I'll miss my train.
unless
I'll .... leave now.

36 Would you like to go for a coffee in 10 minutes or so?
about
How .... a coffee in 10 minutes or so?

37 It seems to me that her playing has developed amazingly in the past year.
seems
Her playing .... in the past year.

38 Thanks for reminding me about this meeting – otherwise I would have missed it.
not
If you .... about this meeting, I would have missed it.

39 I don't normally go into town by car.
used
I .... into town by car.

40 I would like to express my thanks for everything you have done for me.
thankful
I'd like to say .... am for everything you have done for me.

PART 4

For questions **41–55**, read the text below and look carefully at each line. Some of the lines are correct, and some have a word which should not be there.

If a line is correct, put a tick (✓) by the number **on the separate answer sheet**. If a line has a word which should **not** be there, write the word **on the separate answer sheet**. There are two examples at the beginning (**0** and **00**).

Examples:

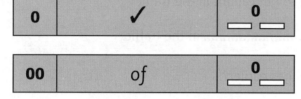

Living to 120?

0   The famous musician, Pablo Casals, tells in his autobiography how he

00 once received of a letter from a special orchestra in a village in the

41 mountains of the Republic of Georgia: the letter has invited him to play

42 with the orchestra. The orchestra was had a rule that only people who

43 were over than 100 years old could play with them. Casals was a

44 'young' man of only 80 at the time, but because he was a such

45 a famous musician, the orchestra decided to make an exception in his

46 case. Casals later found out that the letter was a joke. But who knows –

47 maybe the time will be soon come when it is possible to have such

48 orchestras? The fact is that the average of life expentancy is rising. For

49 example, in Shakespeare's days the very few people lived to be 40.

50 Even as late as 1900, most of people could expect to live only to the age

51 of 50 or so. But a boy born today will probably reach to the age of 75.

52 Women generally live longer than men, so a girl born today will

53 probably live to the age of 80. In the future, people will probably live

54 much more longer than that. So maybe one of us will live long enough to

55 hear an orchestra whose members are all over 100.

PART 5

For questions **56–65**, read the text below. Use the word given in capitals at the end of each line to form a word that fits in the space in the same line. There is an example at the beginning (**0**). Write your word **on the separate answer sheet**.

Example:

0	*impossible*	0

The environment: our responsibility

These days it is **(0)**............... to open a newspaper without reading about the   **POSSIBLE**

damage we are doing to the environment. The earth is being **(56)**............... and   **THREAT**

the future looks bad. What can each of us do?

We cannot clean up our **(57)**............... rivers and seas overnight. Nor can we   **POLLUTION**

stop the **(58)**............... of plants and animals. But we can stop adding to the   **APPEAR**

problem while **(59)**............... search for answers, and laws are passed in   **SCIENCE**

nature's **(60)**............... .   **DEFEND**

It may not be easy to change your lifestyle **(61)**............... , but some steps are   **COMPLETE**

easy to take: cut down the amount of **(62)**............... you do, or use as little plastic   **DRIVE**

as possible. It is also easy to save energy, which also reduces **(63)**............... bills.   **HOUSE**

We must all make a personal **(64)**............... to work for the future of our planet if   **DECIDE**

we want to **(65)**............... a better world for our grandchildren.   **SURE**

Paper 4 – Listening

PART 1

You will hear people talking in eight different situations.
For questions **1–8** choose the best answer, **A**, **B** or **C**.

1   You are in a restaurant and hear a woman talking to a waiter. Why is the customer annoyed?
    A The waiter is behaving rudely.
    B She doesn't have time to eat what she wants.
    C She thinks the restaurant rules are ridiculous.

1

2   You hear this conversation between a man and a secretary about using music practice rooms.
    What will the man be allowed to do?
    A Use the rooms at any time.
    B Use a practice room only after reserving it.
    C Use a room only in the daytime if it is free.

2

3   Listen to this conversation about cooking. Who is talking?
    A Two radio presenters.
    B Two television presenters.
    C Two friends.

3

4   Listen to this woman talking to her friend. What is she asking her friend to do?
    A To come to the theatre.
    B To do some babysitting.
    C To find another babysitter.

4

5   You hear this story on the radio. Why is the passenger telling this story?
    A It is a humorous story about flying.
    B It is a warning not to do illegal things.
    C It is a description of an accident.

5

6   Listen to this man talking about a housing estate. Who is the man?
    A An estate agent.
    B A home owner.
    C An architect.

6

7   You are at the local library and hear a man talking to the librarian. What does the man want?
    A To borrow a book.
    B To renew the loan of a book.
    C To have more books than he is allowed.

7

8   Listen to this woman telling a story. What is she talking about?
    A A film.
    B A play.
    C A book.

8

PART 2

You will hear a man who is looking for a flat talking to an estate agent
about the type of flat that he wants to rent.
For questions **9–18**, fill in the estate agent's form.

Size of flat:	9
Area:	10
Distance from public transport:	11
Furniture wanted: *flat should be*	12
Upper price limit:	13
Starting when?	14
Period:	15
Additional points: *flat must be*	16
preferably	17
and	18

PART 3

You will hear five different women talking about their jobs.
For questions **19–23**, choose from the list **A–F** which kind of job each
person does. Use the letters only once. There is one extra letter which you
do not need to use.

A   a secretary

B   a bank clerk

C   a waitress

D   a librarian

E   a hotel receptionist

F   a shop assistant

Speaker 1 | 19 |

Speaker 2 | 20 |

Speaker 3 | 21 |

Speaker 4 | 22 |

Speaker 5 | 23 |

PART 4

You will hear part of a radio programme about a sports event.
For questions **24–30**, decide which of the choices **A**, **B** or **C** is the correct
answer.

24 What is special about the festival?

    A It is the largest event of its kind.
    B It includes a large number of Fun Sessions.
    C People can both watch and practise sports.

	24

25 Who are the Fun Sessions aimed at?

    A People who have never practised sports before.
    B Sports lovers of all ages.
    C Children who want to try a new sport.

	25

26 Why does the speaker recommend that parents bring their children along to the Fun Sessions?

    A It is a way of involving children in sports.
    B Many children need new sports skills.
    C Many children are not active enough.

	26

27 Which of these sports does the Watersports Activity Course include?

    A Swimming.
    B Rowing.
    C Diving.

	27

28 Numbers on the watersports course are limited because

    A too many people want to try this event.
    B it depends on the availability of equipment.
    C the equipment needed is very expensive.

	28

29 The Fun Run is intended for

    A people invited to take part.
    B people who like competitions.
    C everyone who likes running.

	29

30 Who is this talk aimed at?

    A People who have bought tickets for events.
    B People who may not have heard about the event.
    C Parents of children who have registered.

	30

Paper 5 – Speaking

The photographs and pictures the interlocutor refers to appear on pages 123–125.

PART 1

The interlocutor encourages each of the candidates in turn to give personal information about themselves by asking questions such as:

Where are you from?
How long have you lived here/there?
What is it like living here/there?
How do you usually spend your free time?
What are your plans for the future?

PART 2

The interlocutor gives each of the candidates in turn two photographs to look at and gives the following instructions:

Candidate A, here are your two pictures. Please let Candidate B see them. They show two different classrooms. Candidate A, I'd like you to compare and contrast these pictures saying how you feel about classrooms like these. When Candidate A has finished, I'd like you, Candidate B, to tell us which classroom seems more attractive to you.

* * *

Candidate B, here are your two pictures. Please let Candidate A see them. They show two different types of social occasion. Candidate B, I'd like you to compare and contrast these pictures saying how you feel about these types of social occasion. When Candidate B has finished, I'd like you, Candidate A, to tell us which social occasion you would prefer to be invited to.

PART 3

The interlocutor gives the candidates some illustrations to look at and gives the following instructions:

Now, Candidates A and B, I am going to show you a series of drawings which tell a story. The illustrations are in a scrambled order. I'd like you to talk to each other and decide together what the correct order of the illustrations is.

PART 4

The interlocutor encourages the candidates to develop the topic raised in Part 3 by asking questions such as:

Have you ever left anything important behind?
Are you forgetful?
What do people sometimes do in order not to forget to do things?
What would you do if you were in place of the man in the pictures and you realised you had left your briefcase at home?

Practice exam 5

Paper 1 – Reading

PART 1

You are going to read an article about children who spend too much time at the computer. Choose the most suitable heading from the list **A–I** for each part (**1–7**) of the article. There is one extra heading which you do not need to use. There is an example at the beginning (**0**).
Mark your answers **on the separate answer sheet**.

A	When the problem disappears.
B	Teachers – watch for the signs!
C	How the habit is broken.
D	The extent of the problem.
E	Parents on the lookout.
F	Stop those computers now!
G	How affected children act.
H	The type of child at risk.
I	Our children are in danger!

A price to pay

Danger when a computer becomes your best friend

0 **I**

Many of Britain's children are becoming computer addicts, according to leading education specialists. Such children then lose interest in anything else and become withdrawn and introverted.

1

Up to one in ten youngsters – over half a million – are affected. The problem usually starts between the ages of nine and eleven and most often affects boys, who tend to get more involved with machines than girls. They spend up to 40 hours a week tapping away.

2

'These children are unable to relate to friends and family or express their feelings,' says Mrs Noel Janis-Norton, a specialist at treating problem children and adults. They behave badly at school and at home – and when desperate parents forbid them to use computers, they find ways to use the computers in secret and deceive their parents. The result is that they often fail school tests and lose friends. But they do not care. The computer has become their best – and sometimes their only – friend.

3

Mrs Janis-Norton says children who have difficulty communicating are hit by this problem. 'A child who is energetic and outgoing is unlikely to become a computer addict, although any kind of child can enjoy the computer,' she says. 'There's a very big difference between use and abuse. Often the problem continues into the late teens and sometimes into adult life, where the addict becomes increasingly shut off from reality.'

4

Mrs Janis-Norton adds: 'The situation changes when they have less to be anxious about. Many grow out of it when they leave home. Like any other nervous condition, such as asthma, it hardly exists in the summer holidays.'

5

Most children who have this kind of nervous complaint are not doing as well at school as they could. Now teachers are being asked to look for the more obvious patterns of behaviour. The National Union of Teachers has already warned its staff to identify pupils who become restless and agitated.

6

Tony Miller, one of the teachers' union spokesmen, says parents should limit the amount of time their children spend at the machines. He adds: 'Very young children take to computers like fish to water. It seems to be like the problem of obsessive TV-watching.' One parent was woken at 5 a.m. by a strange bleeping noise. She later discovered it was her addict son at his computer.

7

Mrs Janis-Norton claims a high success rate with her unique system which involves teaching the parents as well as the child. It is a similar problem to gambling or drug addiction. She says: 'With the parents, we examine all the issues that come up in a child's day – food, bedtime, co-operation, homework, the tone of voice children use when talking to their parents, and sweets. We teach parents how to be in charge of the situation, how to be positive, firm and consistent. We give the child extra lessons in whatever subjects they're weak in. By slowly getting the children off the machines, and replacing computers with other activities and more confidence, the habit is broken.'

PART 2

You are going to read a text about sailing around the world with children on board. For questions **8–14**, choose the answer (**A, B, C** or **D**) which you think fits best according to the text.

Mark your answers **on the separate answer sheet**.

When we first took our two children to sea with us, it was rare to come across other families on sailing boats. Usually such meetings resulted in the children quickly making friends,
5 while we parents discussed how we managed. At first, I was worried about taking children to sea and I had many questions. How would I amuse them? What if they fell ill at sea? Added to such questions was the major problem of
10 their education. When we set out on our voyage, my daughter was seven, my son five, and we planned to sail for three years. That we only returned to England six years later with 60,000 miles behind us and children of thirteen
15 and eleven years old, is an indication of how my worries had been answered. One change over these years has been the increase in the number of parents who take their children to sea on long voyages. Thus what I shall be
20 saying here and in later chapters is based not only on my own experiences, but also on those of others, many of whom have taken their children cruising around the world.

Those experiences show that although there
25 are problems and worries in taking children on cruises, they are not insurmountable and can be solved with some thought and careful planning. The same basic principles apply at sea as on land. Careful parents take precautions to
30 avoid accidents in the home, and should behave the same way on a boat. Few people would let a small child alone near a busy road, without being convinced that the child was aware of the dangers of traffic. Similarly most
35 parents do not let non-swimmers near water alone or without protection. Water safety has many parallels with road safety and, regarded as such, it is simply commonsense to teach children to live near water safely.
40 There are also benefits in taking children to sea. In our society we are in great danger of

making life too easy for our children. A certain amount of stress is necessary for every child's development. Overprotection can damage a
45 child's personality and prevent the development of independence. Sailing is one way of providing some stress and limited hardship, which will help to build the child's character. Thoughts such as these played an
50 important part in our decision to take our children on a voyage around the world.

One of the differences between living on a boat and living ashore is that fathers are usually much more involved with their children than they
55 are ashore. As Liz MacDonald, who sailed around the world with her son Jeff, explained to me, 'At sea, Jeff saw his father actually working, solving problems under stress, such as when gear broke in heavy weather. Before we went sailing he only
60 saw his father for a short time at the end of each day. Now they have a much stronger relationship.' The closeness between parents and children on boats arises out of the fact that the child often witnesses a parent dealing with a difficult
65 problem or an emergency. In a squall or bad weather, a child will have to learn that the safety of the boat, and thus the safety of the family, is more important than minor demands or fears of the child. Learning that getting the sail down
70 quickly comes first can lead to the child considering the needs of others as well as himself.

If one expects to get fun out of sailing with children, one is likely to find it fun. Still, there are many things to be considered before the
75 fun starts and those I shall be examining in later chapters, from the safety and health of children on board to practical suggestions for amusing children at sea. Above all, remember throughout that cruising with children can be
80 enjoyable and is not so difficult. It can also be of great benefit to the children themselves. So let's go cruising!

8   The writer's family sailed for six years because

  A   the route took longer than they thought.
  B   the children made friends with other children.
  C   the attitude to sailing with children has changed.
  D   they had been able to solve the problems with the children.

9   What does the writer say about living at sea and on land?

  A   Taking children to sea is more dangerous.
  B   They require the same general outlook.
  C   Living at sea requires more commonsense.
  D   Knowing road safety means knowing water safety.

10 The word 'they' in line 26 refers to

  A   problems and worries.
  B   children.
  C   experiences.
  D   cruises.

11 One of the reasons the writer took her children to sea was

  A   to teach and educate them herself.
  B   to protect them as much as possible.
  C   to show them the world.
  D   to help them develop as individuals.

12 The word 'squall' in line 65 means

  A   fight.
  B   storm.
  C   boat.
  D   fear.

13 From living on a boat children learn

  A   to love their parents more.
  B   to behave like their fathers.
  C   to be less selfish.
  D   to repair sailing equipment.

14 This passage is taken from

  A   an introduction to a book.
  B   a book review.
  C   an interview.
  D   an article on sailing.

PART 3

You are going to read a magazine article about a rail journey. Eight sentences have been removed from the article. Choose from the sentences **A–I** the one which fits each gap (**15–21**). There is one extra sentence which you do not need to use. There is an example at the beginning (**0**).
Mark your answers **on the separate answer sheet**.

From Dundee to Penzance

You've got to be quite keen to be prepared to spend 12 hours on a train going somewhere you really don't want to go. But that's what we were doing as we left Dundee one grey, wet, spring morning. With any luck, 12 hours, 20 counties, and 689 miles later, we would be in Penzance, in Cornwall, which is the furthest you can travel in Britain without changing trains. And because we were going to Cornwall, the train is appropriately called 'The Cornishman'.

No sooner had we left than we were crossing the river Tay. **0** **I** The replacement, which opened eight years later, is Europe's longest rail bridge.

15 While the first one, the Tay Bridge, reminds travellers of the failings of engineers, the magnificent Forth Bridge outside Edinburgh, which was opened in 1890, stands as a monument to Scottish engineers.

The train picked up speed as we left Edinburgh behind. We passed through the wooded hills of the Borders, and then suddenly the hills fell away, and we were looking straight down on to a rocky bay and harbour. **16** We decided it was time for breakfast.

On 'The Cornishman', passengers travelling very long distances get an unlimited supply of tea and coffee and two free meals. **17** While eating our breakfast, we enjoyed the views of the coastline.

18 The Royal Border Bridge, with its 28 stone arches, was opened by Queen Victoria in 1850. Despite the name, the border between Scotland and England actually lies a couple of miles to the north.

Nothing special happened as we sped from the north through most of England. After Exeter, we saw the sea for the first time since the north and we soon entered Cornwall over the fourth famous bridge, the Royal Albert Bridge. Its two huge spans were built high enough over the River Tamar to allow the Navy's ships to pass beneath.

By now there were few passengers aboard. Progress was slow, the 80 miles from Plymouth to Penzance taking two hours. **19** One minute we would be passing through a cutting, the next we would seem to be gliding high above a steep-sided wooded valley.

'The Cornishman' had taken us through a large portion of Scotland, and from the most northerly point in England, to nearly the most southerly. We had experienced rain, sun, and mist. We also seemed to have passed between seasons; in Scotland the spring flowers were just blooming, in Cornwall they had already faded. **20**

We arrived at Penzance two minutes early. Wearily, we stepped on to the platform. The stewards were unloading the remains of the food and drink. **21** Tomorrow they would be working 'The Cornishman' back north. Much as we'd enjoyed taking Britain's longest train journey, it was not an experience we wished to repeat quite so soon.

A   We were on time, nearly six and a half hours into the journey, having covered 393 miles.

B   At Berwick-upon-Tweed we crossed the third great bridge.

C   But the line was breathtakingly beautiful.

D   They had been on their feet the whole time, but had managed to remain cheerful.

E   But in spite of all this, it hadn't been a terribly exciting journey.

F   It was nearly 9 a.m., and as we had already been travelling for two hours, we were getting hungry.

G   'The Cornishman' is unique in being the only regularly scheduled passenger train to cross Britain's four most famous railway bridges.

H   Unfortunately, they do not have a proper kitchen on board, so our food had been microwaved, but it was served on a china plate.

I   The remains of the old bridge still stick up out of the water, a reminder of the disaster in 1879.

PART 4

You are going to read a magazine interview with five woman MPs (Members of Parliament).

For questions **22–35** choose from the list of women (**A–E**) in the box. Some of the women may be chosen more than once. When more than one answer is required, these may be given in any order. There is an example at the beginning (**0**).

Mark your answers **on the separate answer sheet**.

A	Edwina Currie	**D**	Tessa Jowell
B	Harriet Harman	**E**	Anne Coffey
C	Diana Maddock		

Which of the women MPs:

is also a writer? **0** **A**

complain about the attitude of male MPs to women? **22** ☐ **23** ☐

think there will be no problem with female MPs in the future? **24** ☐ **25** ☐

mention women's difficulties in other areas as well? **26** ☐ **27** ☐

thinks it is an advantage to be an older woman in Parliament? **28** ☐

complains about the arrangements for children in Parliament? **29** ☐

feels female MPs work together more than men do? **30** ☐

feels that her work has harmed her family? **31** ☐

thinks Parliament should change fundamentally? **32** ☐

thinks male and female MPs face the same type of difficulty? **33** ☐

live near the Houses of Parliament? **34** ☐ **35** ☐

Is there a woman in the house?

Women have been taking up seats in Parliament since 1920. Sharon Garfinkle talks to female MPs about the pressure and prejudice they still face today.

Edwina Currie

This place is full of people whose way of thinking is amazingly old-fashioned. When my novel was published, I was talking to a journalist friend when a male colleague came and put his arm around me. I introduced him to the journalist and the MP said: 'I've always said we shouldn't have women in this place. They aren't suited for it. They ought to be at home looking after the children.' The journalist's mouth dropped open. My own feeling is that when we get 200 women here, this tone will disappear.

Being a Parliamentarian is a very demanding job. It means conflict between home and occupation for both men and women. It is no ordinary job – you must have a huge amount of commitment and energy.

Harriet Harman

If Parliament is to include women, it has to be run in a different way. The issues for me are different to the issues for male MPs because they might have a wife who's taking responsibility for their children, whereas I don't. I became a new MP and a new mother at more or less the same time. Both of these were overwhelming experiences. One of the critical things for me is that my constituency and home are in London and only 15 minutes from the Houses of Parliament.

In the future women in Parliament will not be an issue. We'll be here in equal numbers and on equal terms.

Diana Maddock

I knew that Parliament would be a strange place and I would be surrounded by arrogant men, but the reality was 20 times worse. Gaining my seat has been quite an upheaval. I have a pager, so my two teenage daughters can always get a message to me. As I've become more involved with politics over the years it has played a greater part in their life. But they both did well in their exams this year, so it can't have affected them academically.

During my campaign newspapers described me as a 'nice, grey-haired granny type'. Yet I see these characteristics as being important as it means I can relate to people.

Tessa Jowell

I do feel fortunate that I am a London MP and live at home. My little boy is very interested in politics and likes coming along. But it's not a building which is terribly well organised for children. There's only one family room. I manage because my husband is incredibly supportive.

What I'm doing is what so many women up and down the country are doing with no recognition at all. It is a fact that as women increasingly combine home and career they are coming under pressure to strike a balance between the two jobs. There are some wonderful women in Parliament and I think we're working co-operatively more and more. That's something women are better at doing than men.

Anne Coffey

I think my career has made life very difficult for my 17-year-old daughter. She was 14 when I was elected and it was very disruptive for her since I had to leave her during the week. Her exam results were terrible and I'm convinced that if she had had a more stable situation, she would have done better.

I think it's very difficult to escape from this type of guilt if you are a woman, but if I hadn't become a politician and stayed at home I would simply have ended up reproducing my mother's life. If you put your children first, then you limit the world for yourself.

Nothing prepares you for the complexity and enormity of this place, and I had problems at first due to ignorance of how things work.

Paper 2 – Writing

PART 1

You **must** answer this question.

1 You have seen the advertisement below for a cruise* on the river Ore, and are interested in going on such a cruise with a number of friends. Using the advertisement and the notes you have made, write a letter to the cruise organisers asking for more information.

LADY FLORENCE
Lunch or dinner cruises

Can we stop? Make small changes?

From Orford we cruise upriver past Aldeburgh to within sight of Iken and Snape. We return past Havergate Island, turning at Shingle Street.

The lunch cruise is from 12 noon to 4 pm. Dinner cruises are on summer evenings from April to September.

Your meal is freshly prepared on board, typically:
Smoked Mackerel Paté
Roast Leg of Lamb
Chocolate Mousse

*Choice?
Vegetables?
Vegetarian meals?*

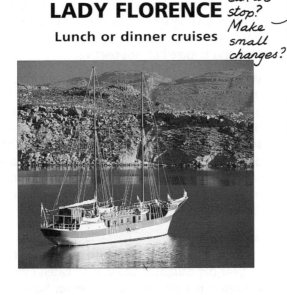

The river

Orfordness

Aldeburgh — *Stop and visit?*

River Alde

Orford Quay *Lady Florence* sails from here — *Can we stop and get off?*

Havergate Island

Iken

Yarn Hill Orford Castle

River Ore

N

The cruise

Lady Florence cruises within the Rivers Alde and Ore for hours during which lunch or dinner is served.

The cruise operates all year round, regardless of weather and tides, taking just twelve passengers.

What if there are 13 of us?

Booking information

The four hour cruise is £9.00 per person *Reduction for parties?*

The cruise is ideally suited for birthdays, anniversaries, naturalists, ornithologists, family or club outings and office parties.

Call: *Lady Florence* cruises, 01798 465216

Write a **letter** of between **120 and 180** words in an appropriate style. Do not write any addresses.

* **cruise**: a trip on a ship or boat for pleasure rather than in order to reach a particular destination

PART 2

Write an answer to **one** of the questions **2–5** in this part. Write your answer in **120–180** words in an appropriate style.

2   An International Youth Magazine is conducting a survey on the typical ways in which young people around the world spend their summer vacation.

Write an **article** for the magazine about what most young people in your country do in the summer.

3   Your teacher has asked your group to consider the advantages and disadvantages of having a part-time job and write a composition answering the question:

Should teenagers take part-time jobs during the school year?

Write your **composition**.

4   You have seen the advertisement below and have decided to apply for one of the trainee positions.

TRAIN FOR A CAREER IN THE RESTAURANT BUSINESS!

Ed's Eatery has vacancies for trainee cooks, waiters, and managers.

Applicants should enjoy working with people and
have some previous experience working in a restaurant.
Fluency in foreign languages essential: most of our customers are tourists.

APPLICATIONS, IN WRITING, TO **ED'S EATERY**, 35 North Street, Cardiff.

Write your **letter of application**. Do not write any addresses.

5   **Background reading texts**

Answer **one** of the following two questions based on your reading of **one** of the set books.

(a)   Describe one or two of the scenes in the book which surprised you. Explain briefly what happened, why you were surprised, and why you think the author included these scenes in the book.

(b)   You have been asked to contribute to a magazine column called *Would you read this book again?*, in which contributors explain why they would – or would not – read a book of their choice a second time.

Write your **composition** for this column.

Paper 3 – Use of English

PART 1

For questions **1–15**, read the text below and decide which word **A**, **B**, **C** or **D** best fits each space. There is an example at the beginning (**0**).
Mark your answers **on the separate answer sheet**.

Example:

0 **A** bought   **B** got   **C** took   **D** shopped

0	A	B	C	D
	▬	▭	▭	▭

The best stone in the world

In 1769 George and Eleanor Coade **(0)**..... a factory manufacturing artificial stone in south-east London on a **(1)**..... at Pedlar's Acre, south **(2)**..... the river. The family were **(3)**..... running a successful factory in the south-west of England. Within a year of moving **(4)**..... the capital, George Coade died, leaving his wife and daughter to **(5)**..... on the business. The Coade Stone they perfected **(6)**..... to become the most permanent stone ever made. The product developed by the factory's former **(7)**..... , Richard Holt, was a kind of baked clay. The two women **(8)**..... with his recipe, and **(9)**..... in creating a new kind of stone which was almost a hundred percent weather-proof.

The advantage of Coade Stone is that while natural stone slowly breaks down and erodes away, Coade Stone seems to be **(10)**..... to survive in all weather conditions for many years. The National Gallery, the Royal Opera House and Buckingham Palace **(11)**..... display their original ornaments made of Coade Stone. **(12)**..... mother and daughter were clever businesswomen. They **(13)**..... only the top artists of the day to model their stone into statues and other ornaments.

After the deaths of Eleanor Coade and her daughter the factory survived for twenty years, but in 1840 it **(14)**..... closed. With it went the Coade Stone recipe which was **(15)**..... , and has never been rediscovered.

1	**A** territory	**B** place	**C** ground	**D** plot
2	**A** to	**B** of	**C** from	**D** than
3	**A** already	**B** just	**C** yet	**D** however
4	**A** at	**B** in	**C** to	**D** on
5	**A** go	**B** carry	**C** get	**D** run
6	**A** claimed	**B** had	**C** was	**D** would

7	A	landlord	B	possessor	C	owner	D	tenant
8	A	experimented	B	tried	C	experienced	D	tested
9	A	managed	B	succeeded	C	achieved	D	completed
10	A	capable	B	possible	C	able	D	good
11	A	still	B	only	C	just	D	yet
12	A	Either	B	Also	C	Each	D	Both
13	A	employed	B	worked	C	staffed	D	teamed
14	A	lastly	B	at last	C	in the end	D	finally
15	A	missing	B	disappeared	C	lost	D	left

PART 2

For questions **16–30**, read the text below and think of the word which best fits each space. Use only **one** word in each space. There is an example at the beginning (**0**).

Write your word **on the separate answer sheet**.

Example:

0	*has*	0 ▭ ▭

Television and reading

Many people believe that watching television **(0)**............... resulted in lower reading standards in schools. **(16)**............... , the link between television and printed books is not as simple as that. In many **(17)**............... , television actually encourages people to read: for example, when a book is turned into a TV series, **(18)**............... sales often go up.

One study of this link examined six-year-old children who **(19)**............... viewing a special series of 15-minute programmes at school. The series was designed to encourage love of books, as **(20)**............... as to develop the basic mechanical skills of reading. Each programme is an animated film of a children's book. The story is read aloud **(21)**............... certain key phrases from the book appear on the screen, beneath the picture. Whenever a word is read, it is also highlighted on the TV screen.

One finding was **(22)**............... watching these programmes was very important to the children. If anything prevented them **(23)**............... seeing a programme, they were very disappointed. What's more, they wanted to read the books **(24)**............... the different parts of the series were based on.

The programmes also gave the children **(25)**............... confidence when looking at these books. As a result of **(26)**............... familiarity with the stories, they would sit in pairs and read the stories aloud to **(27)**............... other. On **(28)**............... occasion, the children showed great sympathy when discussing a character in a book because they themselves **(29)**............... been moved when watching the character **(30)**............... television.

PART 3

For questions **31–40**, complete the second sentence so that it has a similar meaning to the first sentence, using the word given. **Do not change the word given**. You must use between two and five words, including the word given. There is an example at the beginning. (**0**)
Write **only** the missing words **on the separate answer sheet**.

Example:

0   I was unable to be here on time because of the traffic.
     it
     If .... the traffic, I would have been here on time.

     The gap can be filled by the words 'it had not been for', so you write:

0	it had not been for

31   They decided to build a new school immediately.
     should
     They decided that a .... immediately.

32   He had a very traditional upbringing, didn't he?
     traditionally
     He .... , wasn't he?

33   I go out very little these days.
     hardly
     I .... days.

34   My parents were always telling me what to do when I was small.
     being
     I .... to do when I was small.

35   She seemed quite unhappy when I saw her last week.
     look
     When I saw her last week, ... at all.

36   'Could I borrow five pounds from you, Rose?' asked Nick.
     lend
     Nick asked Rose if .... five pounds.

37   There's no way we can agree to this solution.
     question
     This solution .... as far as we are concerned.

38 I didn't have enough time to visit the town properly.
too
The time I had .... the town properly.

39 Although I warned them not to climb that tree, they did.
warning
In spite of .... tree.

40 There aren't many people who have read this novel to the end, but John is one of them.
few
John is .... who have read this novel to the end.

PART 4

For questions **41–55**, read the text below and look carefully at each line.
Some of the lines are correct, and some have a word which should not
be there.
If a line is correct, put a tick (✓) by the number **on the separate answer
sheet**. If a line has a word which should **not** be there, write the word
on the separate answer sheet. There are two examples at the beginning
(**0** and **00**).

Examples:

Life is a *Cabaret*

0 When I was a teenager in the New York, I bought tickets for the
00 musical *Cabaret* with the famous actress Lotte Lenya. But that
41 weekend I had to visit friends in a town far away, and was going
42 to fly back and arrive in time to see the musical. Unfortunately,
43 that night there was a very huge snowstorm and when I got to the
44 airport, I found it out that the flight had been cancelled. But my
45 girlfriend and I were supposed to meet us at the theatre, and I had
46 the tickets! Luckily, two of the passengers on the flight decided that
47 they would rent a car and drive, so I joined to them. But it was
48 being clear that I would not make it to the play on time. I tried to
49 call my girlfriend, but she had already left the home!
50 I got to the theatre during the interval in the play. I went in and
51 my girlfriend she was sitting in her seat! I asked her how
52 she had got in. She said that she started to getting very
53 worried when she realised I was late. She thought that it would
54 be stupid to wait me outside, so she went to the box office and
55 luckily they were able to tell her which seats I had bought them
   and they let her in. So at least one of us saw the whole musical!

PART 5

For questions **56–65**, read the text below. Use the word given in capitals at the end of each line to form a word that fits in the space in the same line. There is an example at the beginning (**0**). Write your word **on the separate answer sheet**.

Example: | **0** | commercial | **0** __ __ |

The history of fishing

(0).............. fishing has been carried out since the middle ages. Before   **COMMERCE**

that it was **(56)**.............. to keep fish for long periods, but the   **POSSIBLE**

development of **(57)**.............. methods such as drying and salting   **STORE**

made it possible for **(58)**.............. to go on fishing trips further away.   **FISH**

In fact, although Europeans were completely **(59)**.............. of   **AWARE**

America's **(60)**.............. , they were already fishing near its coasts   **EXIST**

then. They were, however, still **(61)**.............. to keep fish fresh for any   **ABILITY**

(62).............. of time.   **LONG**

All this changed as a result of the new **(63)**.............. advances in   **TECHNOLOGY**

refrigeration in the 19th century. Soon the **(64)**.............. waters of   **COAST**

Africa and the Mediterranean were full of Northern European fishing

boats. In the 20th century, scientific **(65)**.............. made during the   **DISCOVER**

Second World War were used for discovering large groups of fish.

Paper 4 – Listening

PART 1

You will hear people talking in eight different situations.
For questions **1–8** choose the best answer, **A**, **B** or **C**.

1   You are at a party when you hear two people talk. What is the relationship between the two speakers?
    A   They know each other well.
    B   They are acquaintances but not friends.
    C   They have just met for the first time.

        1

2   Listen to this conversation between two speakers who are disturbed by a noise.
    What is making this noise?
    A   A police siren.
    B   A car alarm.
    C   A burglar alarm.

        2

3   Listen to this man talking on the phone about a lunchtime party he did not go to.
    Why did the man not go?
    A   He didn't want to miss lunch.
    B   He forgot about the party.
    C   He didn't feel like going.

        3

4   Listen to these two people discussing the arrangements for a meeting.
    Where will the meeting be held?
    A   In the new offices.
    B   In the man's office.
    C   In the woman's office.

        4

5   Listen to this reporter talking on a radio programme. What is the main topic of this programme?
    A   The weather.
    B   What to do at the weekend.
    C   Art galleries.

        5

6   Listen to this conversation between a tourist and a woman at a train station.
    What platform is the tourist going to go to?
    A   Platform 5.
    B   Platform 8.
    C   Platform 10.

        6

7   Listen to this woman telling a friend about a cookbook that she bought.
    What does she like about the book?
    A   She likes the variety of recipes.
    B   It will help her lose weight.
    C   The photographs are excellent.

        7

8   Listen to this man talking about riding bicycles. What is the main point he is making?
    A   It is the best way to get around town.
    B   Drivers should take more account of cyclists.
    C   Cyclists should learn to cycle carefully.

        8

PART 2

You will hear a woman being interviewed about her film-watching habits.
For questions **9–18**, complete the questionnaire which the interviewer fills
in. You will need to write a word or a short phrase in each box.

Member of Film Club?	Not since	9
What would make you join or re-join the club?		10
Preferred place to see films?		11
Date of last visit to the club?		12
Film seen on last visit?		13
Frequency of visits?		14
Type of film you would like to see more?		15
Which type of advert have you noticed most?		16
Location of adverts noticed?		17
	and	18

PART 3

You will hear five different men talk about why they are learning a new language. For questions **19–23**, choose from the list **A–F** which reason each person mentions. Use the letters only once. There is one extra letter which you do not need to use.

A   He is learning the language for the fun of it.

B   He is going to visit a foreign country.

C   He is learning the language of the country where he lives.

D   His company is sending him abroad to work.

E   He wants to read literature in the foreign language.

F   He wants a better chance of finding a job.

Speaker 1	19
Speaker 2	20
Speaker 3	21
Speaker 4	22
Speaker 5	23

PART 4

You will hear a talk about a new bridge that is going to be built. For questions **24–30**, decide whether the statement in the question is True or False. If it is True, write **T** on your answer sheet. If it is False, write **F** on your answer sheet.

24   The speaker says that the campaign was unpleasant and unfair. **24**

25   In the short term, building the bridge will make no change to the town centre. **25**

26   Most of the new traffic will probably be commercial. **26**

27   The committee saw the financial advantages of developing a new route. **27**

28   Traffic on the north-south route after the bridge is built will be ten times the present volume. **28**

29   In the long term the town centre will develop into a major attraction in the area. **29**

30   The speaker thinks the bridge should be built for economic reasons. **30**

Paper 5 – Speaking

The photographs and pictures the interlocutor refers to appear on pages 126–128.

PART 1

The interlocutor encourages each of the candidates in turn to give personal information about themselves by asking questions such as:

Where are you from?
How long have you lived here/there?
What is it like living here/there?
How do you usually spend your free time?
What are your plans for the future?

PART 2

The interlocutor gives each of the candidates in turn two photographs to look at and gives the following instructions:

Candidate A, here are your two pictures. Please let Candidate B see them. They show different street performers. Candidate A, I'd like you to compare and contrast these pictures saying how you feel about performers like these. When Candidate A has finished, I'd like you, Candidate B, to tell us which of the two you would stop and watch or listen to, and why.

* * *

Candidate B, here are your two pictures. Please let Candidate A see them. They show two different living rooms. Candidate B, I'd like you to compare and contrast these pictures saying how you feel about living rooms like these. When Candidate B has finished, I'd like you Candidate A, to tell us which room seems more attractive to you.

PART 3

The interlocutor gives the candidates some illustrations to look at and gives the following instructions:

Now, Candidates A and B, I'd like you to imagine that you are members of a team in a competition. The rules of the competition allow you to choose the prize for which you will be competing. Here are illustrations of the possible prizes. You have to choose the three prizes you would like to win, in order of preference. The prizes all have the same value, and the competition rules say that you are not allowed to sell the prize that you win.

PART 4

The interlocuter encourages the candidates to develop the topic raised in Part 3 by asking questions such as:

Have you ever taken part in a competition or a quiz show? If you have, did you enjoy it? Did you win anything?
Would you take part in a competition if you were asked to? Why?/Why not?
Have you ever bought lottery tickets? Did you win anything?
What would you do if you won a large amount of money in the lottery or on the pools?

CAMBRIDGE
EXAMINATIONS, CERTIFICATES AND DIPLOMAS
ENGLISH AS A FOREIGN LANGUAGE

University of Cambridge
Local Examinations Syndicate
International Examinations

For Supervisor's use only

If the candidate is ABSENT or has WITHDRAWN mark here

X

Examination Details	9999/01	99/D99
Examination Title	First Certificate in English	
Centre/Candidate No.	AA999/9999	
Candidate Name	A.N. EXAMPLE	

- Sign here if the details above are correct.
....
- Tell the Supervisor now if the details above are not correct.

Candidate Answer Sheet: FCE Paper 1 Reading

Use a pencil

Mark ONE letter for each question.

For example, if you think **B** is the right answer to the question, mark your answer sheet like this:

Change your answer like this:

1	A B C D E F G H I
2	A B C D E F G H I
3	A B C D E F G H I
4	A B C D E F G H I
5	A B C D E F G H I

6	A B C D E F G H I
7	A B C D E F G H I
8	A B C D E F G H I
9	A B C D E F G H I
10	A B C D E F G H I
11	A B C D E F G H I
12	A B C D E F G H I
13	A B C D E F G H I
14	A B C D E F G H I
15	A B C D E F G H I
16	A B C D E F G H I
17	A B C D E F G H I
18	A B C D E F G H I
19	A B C D E F G H I
20	A B C D E F G H I

21	A B C D E F G H I
22	A B C D E F G H I
23	A B C D E F G H I
24	A B C D E F G H I
25	A B C D E F G H I
26	A B C D E F G H I
27	A B C D E F G H I
28	A B C D E F G H I
29	A B C D E F G H I
30	A B C D E F G H I
31	A B C D E F G H I
32	A B C D E F G H I
33	A B C D E F G H I
34	A B C D E F G H I
35	A B C D E F G H I

© UCLES/K&J

CAMBRIDGE
EXAMINATIONS, CERTIFICATES AND DIPLOMAS
ENGLISH AS A FOREIGN LANGUAGE

University of Cambridge
Local Examinations Syndicate
International Examinations

Examination Details	9999/03	99/D99
Examination Title	First Certificate in English	
Centre/Candidate No.	AA999/9999	
Candidate Name	A.N. EXAMPLE	

For Supervisor's use only

If the candidate is ABSENT or has WITHDRAWN mark here

• Sign here if the details above are correct.

....

• Tell the Supervisor now if the details above are not correct.

Candidate Answer Sheet: FCE Paper 3 Use of English

Use a pencil

For **Part 1:** Mark ONE letter for each question.

For example, if you think **C** is the right answer to the question, mark your answer sheet like this:

0 A B C
   ▭ ▭ ▭

For **Parts 2, 3, 4** and **5:** Write your answers in the spaces next to the numbers like this:

0   *example*

Part 1		Part 2	
1 A B C D	16		16
2 A B C D	17		17
3 A B C D	18		18
4 A B C D	19		19
5 A B C D	20		20
6 A B C D	21		21
7 A B C D	22		22
8 A B C D	23		23
9 A B C D	24		24
10 A B C D	25		25
11 A B C D	26		26
12 A B C D	27		27
13 A B C D	28		28
14 A B C D	29		29
15 A B C D	30		30

© UCLES/K&J

Part 3		Do not write here		
31		65 0	1	2
32		65 0	1	2
33		65 0	1	2
34		65 0	1	2
35		65 0	1	2
36		65 0	1	2
37		65 0	1	2
38		65 0	1	2
39		65 0	1	2
40		65 0	1	2

SAMPLE

Part 4		Do not write here
41		41
42		42
43		43
44		44
45		45
46		46
47		47
48		48
49		49
50		50
51		51
52		52
53		53
54		54
55		55

Part 5		Do not write here
56		56
57		57
58		58
59		59
60		60
61		61
62		62
63		63
64		64
65		65

CAMBRIDGE
EXAMINATIONS, CERTIFICATES AND DIPLOMAS
ENGLISH AS A FOREIGN LANGUAGE

University of Cambridge
Local Examinations Syndicate
International Examinations

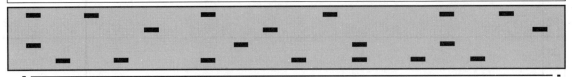

For Supervisor's use only

If the candidate is ABSENT or has WITHDRAWN mark here

X

Examination Details	9999/01	99/D99
Examination Title	First Certificate in English	
Centre/Candidate No.	AA999/9999	
Candidate Name	A.N. EXAMPLE	

- Sign here if the details above are correct.
....
- Tell the Supervisor now if the details above are not correct.

Candidate Answer Sheet: FCE Paper 4 Listening

Mark test version below

A	B	C	D	E

Use a pencil

For **Parts 1** and **3**: Mark ONE letter for each question.

For example, if you think **B** is the right answer to the question, mark your answer sheet like this:

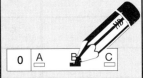

0	A	B	C

For **Parts 2** and **4**: Write your answers in the spaces next to the numbers like this:

0	*example*

Part 1

1	A	B	C
2	A	B	C
3	A	B	C
4	A	B	C
5	A	B	C
6	A	B	C
7	A	B	C
8	A	B	C

Part 3

19	A	B	C	D	E	F
20	A	B	C	D	E	F
21	A	B	C	D	E	F
22	A	B	C	D	E	F
23	A	B	C	D	E	F

Part 2

		Do not write here
9		9
10		10
11		11
12		12
13		13
14		14
15		15
16		16
17		17
18		18

Part 4

		Do not write here
24		24
25		25
26		26
27		27
28		28
29		29
30		30

Visual material for Paper 5

Practice exam 1

Paper 5 – Speaking

PART 2

Candidate A

1

2

Candidate B

1

2

PART 3

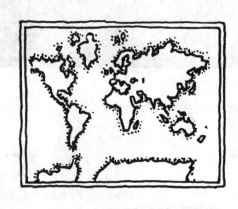

Practice exam 2

Paper 5 – Speaking

PART 2

Candidate A

1

2

Candidate B

PART 3

Practice exam 3

Paper 5 – Speaking

PART 2

Candidate A

1

2

Candidate B

1

2

PART 3

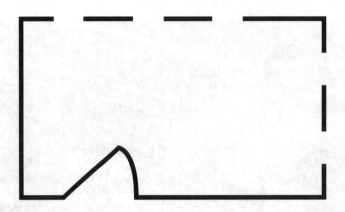

Practice exam 4

Paper 5 – Speaking

PART 2

Candidate A

1

2

Candidate B

1

2

PART 3

a)

b)

c)

d)

e)

f)

Answers: b), e), d), a), c), f).

Practice exam 5

Paper 5 – Speaking

PART 2

Candidate A

1

2

Candidate B

1

2

PART 3

Answer key and tapescripts

Practice exam 1

Paper 1 – Reading

PART 1

1	H
2	G
3	B
4	E
5	A
6	D
7	F

PART 2

8	A
9	B
10	C
11	C
12	A
13	B
14	C

PART 3

15	F
16	E
17	D
18	A
19	G
20	B

PART 4

21	C
22	D
23	B
24	C
25	A
26	D
27	C

28	E
29	B
30	D
31	A
32	D
33	E
34	D
35	C

Paper 3 – Use of English

PART 1

1	B
2	A
3	B
4	A
5	D
6	C
7	D
8	A
9	A
10	B
11	D
12	B
13	A
14	C
15	C

PART 2

16	by
17	to
18	One
19	being
20	to
21	of
22	with
23	than
24	at
25	an
26	during/on
27	well
28	that
29	since/because/as
30	use

PART 3

31	never let me walk
32	must have made her parents
33	apologised for having to
34	never seen such a bad
35	has been living here since
36	made up my mind yet/yet made up my mind
37	finding it increasingly difficult
38	if you stop interrupting
39	you describe her to/for me
40	encouraging him to apply

PART 4

41	✓
42	was
43	for
44	in
45	on
46	that
47	✓
48	✓
49	✓
50	it
51	✓
52	more
53	to
54	in
55	had

PART 5

56	ability
57	repeat
58	produced
59	improvement
60	amazing
61	identify
62	slightly
63	composers
64	musical
65	possibility

Paper 4 – Listening

PART 1

1	A
2	A
3	B
4	B
5	C
6	C
7	C
8	A

PART 2

9	Ann West/Mrs West
10	three kilos/kg of oranges
11	four kilos/kg of peaches
12	£5.24/five pounds twenty-four pence
13	cheque
14	(the) previous order/first order
15	between five and five-thirty/5–5.30
16	the third on the right
17	Monday
18	Tuesday

PART 3

19	C
20	A
21	E
22	D
23	F

PART 4

24	C
25	A
26	B
27	B
28	A
29	C
30	C

Tapescript

Hello. I'm going to give you the instructions for this test. I'll introduce each part of the test and give you time to look at the questions. At the start of each piece you'll hear this sound. (tone) You'll hear each piece twice. Now look at Part 1.

PART 1

You'll hear people talking in eight different situations. For questions 1 to 8, choose the best answer, A, B or C.

Extract 1

I'm terribly sorry I'm late. I don't know why this always happens to me. I'm never able to get anywhere on time. Even if I leave myself plenty of time, I'll do something wrong, like take the wrong bus. But anyway, this time it's really not my fault. There was a terribly long traffic jam on the motorway. We found out later that a car had overturned, though by the time we got there they'd cleared everything.

Extract 2

A: Hello. You left a message in my office saying that you needed to talk to me.

B: Oh, yes. Hello. I'm afraid the airline called and apparently there weren't enough people on the flight, and what they've done is, they're not doing the early flight and they've put the passengers from that flight onto the later flight, which gets you in at nine thirty.

A: But that's too late. I have to be at a meeting at nine.

B: Yes, I'm sorry, but that's what happens with cheap flights.

A: Is there no earlier flight than that?

B: Well, I can look for flights on other airlines, but I checked for someone else this morning and all the seats available were much more expensive.

A: Well, I'll have to take the later flight then, won't I?

Extract 3

You know what happened? I showed him the questions and he said, 'Can you add more questions so that the students have more choice?' So off I went and added two more questions, one for each topic. And then I go in there and we agree on the questions. And after half an hour he comes back to me and says, 'I've decided that they should only have to write three out of the six, two on one topic

and one on the other.' Can you believe it? And frankly, I mean, he can do whatever he likes, but I couldn't tell him what I really thought, could I?

Extract 4

A: Oh dear, I'm not sure this was a good idea.

B: You wouldn't think that this would happen on a day when everyone's going into town and they're advising us to take public transport.

A: Yes, I know. If only they'd let us know. What good are those modern electronic announcement boards if they don't let you know about a cancellation or a late arrival – at least keep you in touch? I told you, we should have taken the bus.

B: Oh, I don't know. At least here once you get going, you know you're safe from traffic jams or accidents.

Extract 5

Right, that was very nice. I liked the way you did the beginning. But you all have to look up – don't forget that you're performing to an audience, and the audience wants to see your eyes. The second point is that you've got to think of the meaning of what you're doing. There are words here – they have meaning. And the meaning of the words is what gives the whole performance its meaning. If we can't understand the words, then we might as well just have the orchestra playing your line. So, can we do this again, looking up, and with meaning?

Extract 6

A: Good afternoon, madam. What can I do for you?

B: Good afternoon. Erm ... I bought this tape recorder here two weeks ago – I'm sure your colleague will remember me – and there is one major problem with it. There seems to be a problem with the speed – and it's not recording well. So I was wondering whether it would be possible to replace it ... erm ... but I'm afraid I don't have my till receipt or the guarantee with me. I only have my credit card slip, so I hope that's alright.

Extract 7

Hello, Mary. There were a number of points which we didn't finalise at our meeting last Monday and which now need immediate attention, I think, if we want this to go through, as I think both of us do. I would appreciate it if you could give me a ring this afternoon so that we can discuss this. I shall be out of the office between twelve and two for a meeting, but otherwise I should be here. Can I stress again that this is beginning to be rather urgent?

Extract 8

Well, when I won the competition to go abroad as an exchange student, it was considered an honour and I thought he was being very supportive. And only later I learnt that he'd actually advised my parents against letting me go. He said that I was having trouble as it was, and I would have great difficulties making up for the material that I would miss. And he was right. But when I had problems later because of the time I'd been away – in fact I nearly failed one subject – he helped me a lot, he intervened and talked to the headmaster and they let me do the exams again.

That's the end of Part 1. Now look at Part 2.

PART 2

You'll hear a woman talking to a grocer ordering food to be delivered to her house. For questions 9 to 18, complete the notes. You'll need to write a word or a short phrase in each box. You now have forty-five seconds in which to look at Part 2.

G = grocer C = customer

G: Hello. Belcher's here. How may I help you?

C: Hello, this is Ann West speaking. Erm ... I put in an order with you about an hour ago, but unfortunately I forgot to order a couple of things I wanted and I was wondering if I could do this now and have everything delivered together.

G: Yes, Mrs West. No problem. Go ahead.

C: OK. Well, I forgot to get oranges, so can I have three kilos of oranges?

G: Yes, no problem.

C: And I'd also like three kilos of pears.

G: Well, for some reason we've actually had very few of those today and we've run out, I'm afraid.

C: Ah. Right. So in that case what should I have instead? Can I have ... erm ... ?

G: Apples maybe? I've got some very nice ...

C: No, no. Not for what I need them ... erm ... I'll use peaches instead. Yes. I'll have four kilos of those.

G: Good. No problem. Plenty of those. Erm, anything else?

C: No – that's it.

G: Good. I'll put the fruit aside for you. That will be five pounds twenty-four pence in all. And you'll be paying by cash as usual?

C: No, I'll be paying by cheque.

G: Fine. Erm, so we'll collect the cheque when we get there. Let me just find the note for your previous order ... yes, here we are. I'll just make a note to deliver both orders together. Is that alright ?

C: Yes, of course. It makes sense to deliver both orders together, but I'd also like to change the time of delivery. I had arranged for delivery at seven, but I'd like to have it earlier. Can you make it at three-thirty?

G: Erm ... I'm afraid there's no one available to make a delivery at that time. But I can ask one of the lads to deliver this between four and five if that's convenient.

C: No, I've got to go out then. In that case ... erm ... can we say between five ... let's say between five and five-thirty. OK?

G: Yes, fine. But in that case can you just remind me again exactly where Swainstone Road is? I mean, I recognise it when I'm there, but now I'll have to give directions to someone. Erm, it's one of the streets on the right immediately after the roundabout, isn't it? When you come from the centre?

C: Yes, it's the third on the right. Oh, yes, and can you make a note asking for the usual delivery next week to be on Monday instead of Tuesday?

G: Yes, no problem.

Now you'll hear Part 2 again.
(Part 2 repeated)
That's the end of Part 2. Now look at Part 3.

PART 3

You'll hear five different people talking about parking cars. They are answering the question: should learner drivers take a parking test? For questions 19 to 23, choose from the list A to F the description that suits each person. Use the letters only once. There is one extra letter which you do not need to use. You now have thirty seconds to look through Part 3.

Speaker 1

It's an excellent idea. As you know, I am the chief examiner at the Institute of Advanced Motorists and I'm sure you know that we include parking in the advanced test because, contrary to what people think, I believe that parking is part of good driving. But people do find it difficult. And also, perhaps it's because men have more knowledge of the mechanics of a car, but for some reason men find reverse parking easier than women. At least they do in my experience.

Speaker 2

I think it's ridiculous. It's not as if being a bad parker means you're a dangerous driver. I'm still not a very good parker, after many years on the road, and I've never had an accident, though I do drive a lot. It's bad enough as it is, what they're asking us to do. We don't really have to be put through all that. What are they trying to produce? Superdrivers?

Speaker 3

In principle, yes, I think we should have a parking test. But of course there are dangers there. Imagine looking out of your window, and some learner comes along, practises parking and backs into your new car. You'd be rather unhappy, wouldn't you? So they'll have to provide special parking practice areas to prevent such accidents, so that there wouldn't be any danger to other cars parked on the road. That would mean that the test would be more expensive and that learning to drive would be more expensive too.

Speaker 4

Yes, I'm afraid I do, but I don't think I would ever have passed the driving test if it had included parking. The problem is that you, you have to do it in a public place, and you get so nervous and stressed that it's a sure way to guarantee an accident. I'm not sure if men really do this better than women. My husband's very good at it, but, well, he ... well, when I'm trying to park, he fires off instructions that are impossible to understand. I always feel that I'm more likely to have an accident while my husband's giving me instructions than at any other time.

Speaker 5

No, but only out of self-interest. I would never have got through if I'd had to park as well. The reason I passed on the seventh attempt was because I took the test in a town where nobody knew me. All the examiners were getting bored with me where I lived. It was terrible every time. Not just my family, the whole town laughed at me. My parking is now the best part of my driving. This doesn't mean I don't hit things from time to time, but it's still good, and I consider myself to be a good parker.

Now you'll hear Part 3 again.
(Part 3 repeated)
That's the end of Part 3. Now look at Part 4.

PART 4

You'll hear an interview with a young couple talking about where they live. For questions 24 to 30, decide which of the choices A, B or C is the correct answer. You now have thirty seconds to look through Part 4.

A = announcer C = Carol S = Steve

A: The next time you can't park anywhere near your house, or find yourself stuck in an overcrowded train, think of the Jacksons. Like many young families, they got sick of living in the big city. They considered moving to the suburbs, but instead they found a small farm and went to live out in a rural area, miles away from the nearest town. And what they did, anyone can do.

C: Well, we were determined to find somewhere we could live, we even thought about going abroad, and then we found this house when we were on holiday.

S: It was actually on the last day staying with Carol's mother.

C: I was determined to find a really nice house to rent. It didn't matter where, so long as it had space for the children and a garden. And once we saw this place we never looked back, though at first living here was really tough. We might even buy this place eventually.

S: We have very fond memories of our early days in London, but in the end I really began to dislike it. I really think London's changed, it's getting worse.

C: And our flat was getting broken into all the time. And you could never get a parking space outside the house, so it was real trouble getting the children from the car into the house. Well, obviously there's more parking space here – acres and acres of it – but that's not the point, is it? What's important is that when I come home and one of the children is asleep, which happens quite often, I can leave him or her in the car because I can see them through the kitchen window, and I know nothing can happen. I leave the car unlocked all night as well.

S: We're not country people, but we're learning. We planted all the lettuces at the same time so we got twenty-four in one weekend!

C: We were eating lettuce for three whole days. You should have seen the children's faces!

S: On the other hand the onions were brilliant, but we didn't grow nearly enough. We'll know better next year.

A: But there are other, more serious problems, aren't there?

S: Yes, well, at the moment the water pipes are in such a state that we can use the water for washing but not to drink.

C: So all the water for cooking and for drinking has to be brought in. We bring huge containers of water from my mother's house.

S: Though, I must say, I don't really mind that. I'm not sure I could actually go back to living in a modern house.

C: Yes, you see, I grew up in a house where we had no electricity and no running water. My parents would be playing cards by candlelight. Houses like that have a special feeling, a special atmosphere, which is lost in big cities, in modern houses.

A: And are you accepted by the local community?

S: Well ... I don't know ...

C: They were quite welcoming in the beginning, showed up with all sorts of goods – we felt great – but that has stopped.

S: Well, I do play football with a few local lads at the weekend.

C: And I am vice-chairman of the local nursery school, in an attempt to get more involved in what's happening around here. But we've still got quite a way to go. Though I must stress again, this is home now.

Now you'll hear Part 4 again.
(Part 4 repeated)
That's the end of Part 4. That's the end of the test.

Practice exam 2

Paper 1 – Reading

PART 1

1 E
2 G
3 D
4 B
5 A
6 C
7 H

PART 2

8 B
9 D
10 B
11 C
12 A
13 A
14 D

PART 3

15 D
16 A
17 B
18 E
19 F
20 G

PART 4

21 D
22 B
23 E
24 C
25 F
26 B
27 B
28 A

29 D
30 F
31 A
32 E
33 B
34 G
35 C

Paper 3 – Use of English

PART 1

1 A
2 C
3 A
4 D
5 A
6 B
7 D
8 B
9 C
10 A
11 B
12 A
13 D
14 B
15 C

PART 2

16 into
17 who
18 make
19 however/though
20 them
21 have/take
22 around/round
23 another (*not* an)
24 which
25 was
26 for
27 Although/Though
28 time/while
29 top
30 being

136

PART 3

31	gave me the most encouragement
32	let down by this
33	so bored by the play
34	(that) he wanted him to
35	would/'d rather you did not/didn't
36	may have forgotten to mention
37	has been ten years since
38	carry on with/doing
39	is not/isn't big/large enough
40	asked Bridget to wait

PART 4

41	✓
42	to
43	✓
44	✓
45	and
46	to
47	he
48	of
49	had
50	been
51	✓
52	to
53	out
54	the
55	himself

PART 5

56	Researchers
57	conclusion
58	development
59	illnesses
60	growing
61	endangered
62	solution
63	carefully
64	differently
65	encouraged

Paper 4 – Listening

PART 1

1	C
2	C
3	A
4	C
5	B
6	A
7	B
8	C

PART 2

9	National Student Union
10	you are/you're a student
11	everywhere/worldwide/ throughout the world/abroad
12	more cheaply/at cheaper rates
13	travel offices
14	the World Travel Handbook
15	cheap hotels
16	legal or medical advice/help
17	£10/ ten pounds
18	3/three passport photos/ photographs

PART 3

19	F
20	B
21	A
22	E
23	D

PART 4

24	J
25	J
26	D
27	A
28	J
29	D
30	A

Tapescript

Hello. I'm going to give you the instructions for this test. I'll introduce each part of the test and give you time to look at the questions. At the start of each piece you'll hear this sound. (tone) You'll hear each piece twice. Now look at Part 1.

PART 1

You'll hear people talking in eight different situations. For questions 1 to 8, choose the best answer, A, B or C.

Extract 1

A: Hello, I'm calling about an appointment for an inspection of the gas pipes. I got a card about it and I was wondering whether you could tell me whether it's in the morning or in the afternoon. My reference number is RG62AA.

B: Right, erm ... well, it doesn't say anything here, so it could be either in the morning or afternoon, depending on the other appointments in the area.

A: Can I have it done in the morning? I need to go out in the afternoon.

B: I'm afraid there's nothing I can do about it now. Would you like me to make another appointment for you, for another morning if you want?

A: Erm, no, no. Let's leave it as it is.

Extract 2

A: Hello. Is John Robertson available or is he teaching?

B: Hello. Are you Mr Spring?

A: Yes, that's right.

B: Well, Mr Robertson's son is ill so he had to fetch him from school and take him home and stay with him. But he said that you could call him there. He's very sorry he's had to cancel again and hopes you won't be too disappointed.

A: Oh dear. I'm sorry to hear about his son, but in fact I dropped in to say that I wouldn't be able to make our meeting this afternoon after all, so in a way I suppose it's good he cancelled.

Extract 3

Drivers are used to changes in traffic mainly because of roadworks, but this morning drivers are advised of changes to traffic for the Reading Marathon Competition, which is taking place this morning between eight and twelve. Shinfield Road is closed from eight to eleven and the Basingstoke Road will be closed to traffic between nine and twelve while runners use these roads at different stages of this exciting event. In addition please note that there has been an accident near the West roundabout, and this is causing some delays.

Extract 4

A: You know Margaret and Stephen?

B: Yes – he's an accountant, right?

A: Yes. Well, he's been offered a senior position in the company here, so they're coming to England.

B: So what's she going to do?

A: Well, she can't really practise here because you've got to take quite a tough exam before you can set up in practice in this country. I think it's given by the Examination Institute for the Medical Professions or something like that. And she has to take it, though of course she got her degree back home and she's been working for years.

B: So what will she do till she passes the exam?

A: She'll probably give private lessons – she speaks Spanish and French.

Extract 5

A: So what are you having today, Tom?

B: Oh, he hasn't decided yet. He always goes round and has a look at what they're serving, even before he takes a tray and plate.

C: Yes, and once I've actually seen what they have, then I decide.

A: Not a very good selection today though, is it?

B: I don't know, I always find something I like, that tastes good and doesn't look too awful.

A: Look at what that man's got – quite a colourful selection, isn't it?

B: Oh, I don't know. I sometimes wish they had one dish on offer and that's it. No need to make decisions.

Extract 6

When I think about how my father behaved with my brother and me, it was actually very touching, because he used to take us to every sporting event in the town. No matter how inappropriate it was, he would take us there. I mean, when there was a basketball game, that was great, but then there were the times when they had boxing on, and I really hated it. The reason he did that was because he felt that it would be good if we went out and did things together, and at that time you didn't get much in our town so he chose whatever he could.

Extract 7

This neighbourhood was built in the 1920s and became a showcase for architects. Each architect had one plot on which to build one house. In spite of this, the neighbourhood has a wonderfully unified style. Look, for example, at the two houses on our left. Now, at the time very few people lived in their own apartments; those flats which existed were small and cramped, had no bathrooms or running water. And here was a massive building project which attempted both to show the different styles in which apartments could be built, and improve living conditions.

Extract 8

Listen, I can't get to sleep because you are making too much noise. And if I can hear you in my room, I'm sure Simon and Tamsin can hear you in theirs and that you're keeping them up as well. So can you be a bit quieter, eh? I've also turned the heating off because I've told you before – it's a waste of money and anyway it's making too much noise roaring away. If you're cold, then go to bed.

That's the end of Part 1. Now look at Part 2.

PART 2

You'll hear part of a talk about an international student organisation. For questions 9 to 18, complete the notes which summarise what the speaker says. You'll need to write a word or a short phrase in each box. You now have forty-five seconds in which to look at Part 2.

A = announcer   H = Hannah

A: And here is Hannah Simon, to talk to us about ISIC – the International Student Identity Card.

H: Good afternoon. If you're a student, you doubtless already belong to a student union – most probably you belong, like most students in the world, to your National Student Union. Through them you probably enjoy a large number of benefits, such as cheaper travel within your country, possibly discounts in many shops, discounts in cinemas and so on. But your National Student Union cards are often not accepted abroad, and in order to get real benefits abroad, you need an ISIC, which stands for International Student Identity Card, which is the only document that is accepted as proof of being a student – and it's accepted not just in some countries in the world, but worldwide. Belonging to ISIC also gives you many benefits that being a member of a National Student Union does not. For example, one important benefit is that you get cheaper air fares on many routes. However, the biggest advantage of becoming an ISIC member is that you gain access to a whole network of student travel offices, a network which is geared especially towards helping people like you. You will appreciate it most when you are going on a long trip, because the arrangements then can be quite complicated. Many students who are going on a trip around the world, for example, need visas and you can use the ISIC office to arrange those. The visa requirements and so on are all listed in the World Travel Handbook, which you get when you join. ISIC travel offices also have a long list of cheap hotels – another important consideration when you are a student trying to save money. Many of our travellers appreciate the special ISIC helpline, which you can call at any time, from anywhere in the world. Although it can help you with various routine, simple enquiries, it's mainly there to assist you in the unfortunate event of your needing legal or medical help.

Becoming a member of ISIC is extremely simple. All you need to do is go to the nearest branch, take three passport photos with you and some money, because an ISIC card costs ten pounds. But although that might sound a lot, in fact you will be saving much more than that by having one.

Now you'll hear Part 2 again.
(Part 2 repeated)
That's the end of Part 2. Now look at Part 3.

PART 3

You'll hear five different people talking about parties they went to. For questions 19 to 23, choose from the list A to F which party each person went to. Use the letters only once. There is one extra letter which you do not need to use. You now have thirty seconds to look through Part 3.

Speaker 1

Well, the nice thing was that the music wasn't too loud, so people could dance and other people could talk. There was a nice mixture of people, and it went on till two in the morning. And apart from the fact that someone spilt half a bottle of coke on my jacket and I had to have it dry cleaned afterwards, everything was fine. Oh yes – and in the middle the stereo stopped playing for some reason, but then after about fifteen minutes it was alright again and we went on dancing.

Speaker 2

Oh, it was great fun and they all enjoyed it. But it was a lot of work, you know, keeping them all happy and making sure they were all behaving themselves, and all taking part in the games we organised and that nobody was feeling left out. And of course there's always someone who misbehaves – and you don't know all the names, which is a problem. But it was nice, nobody misbehaved in any kind of serious way.

Speaker 3

Well, I think it was one of the nicest parties I've ever been to. Janet and Ray have friends who have a huge flat with a very high ceiling. It used to be a warehouse, and these friends let them borrow it for the day. It started at one in the afternoon and then it went on and on and on. And what was nice was that this was the first time that the extended families had met. Of course, his parents and hers had already met, but the rest of the family hadn't. And I think there was this feeling of slight amazement, you know, wow, they've known each other for so many years and they've finally done it!

Speaker 4

It was quite a small affair, I think there were about seven or eight people there in all. We sat in the living room and had coffee and a cake Bridget had baked. She'd got candles and we just sat there and chatted – very pleasant. It started at two or maybe three, I can't remember. I was terribly late because, although it was Sunday, I was working – I had a project I had to finish. And then I realised that I didn't have a present for him, which was terribly embarrassing, but I gave him the present and the card the next day.

Speaker 5

We always have it on the Thursday before they go home. We use one of the old houses on the estate, which has a huge lawn that goes down to the lake. People come at about seven – we just stand there and chat and people wander around. You can really unwind and relax. And it's quite a good atmosphere. People have worked very hard for three weeks and have learned a lot. Of course, we are all adults and there isn't this atmosphere of teacher/student, but there is a bit of distance between them and us because we are working and they're studying. But on the last evening this distance disappears.

Now you'll hear Part 3 again.
(Part 3 repeated)
That's the end of Part 3. Now look at Part 4.

PART 4

You'll hear a conversation between three people who are planning a party: Jill, Andrew and Don. Answer questions 24 to 30 by writing J (for Jill), A (for Andrew) or D (for Don). You now have thirty seconds to look through Part 4.

A = Andrew   J = Jill   D = Don

A: Right. So. Shall we try and find a suitable date for this long-overdue party?

J: How about the second weekend in July, Andrew? That's after all your exams are over, isn't it, so all of your friends will have time. I mean, it doesn't really matter to me, but to you and your friends I suppose it does.

A: Mmm, good thinking, Jill ... yes, sounds OK to me. What do you think, Don?

D: Yes, fine by me. We should have probably thought of it ourselves.

A: Well, we need to decide how big it's going to be, and how many people each of us should invite.

D: Andrew, do we really need to do this? I mean, why don't we just each invite as many people as we like?

A: Well, Don, the point is that we may end up having so many people that we won't have enough food and drink for them. I think you need to think about whether we'd like to invite only close friends, or whether we want to invite lots of people and have this as a noisy, free-for-all type of party.

J: Well, I have a lot of people I'd like to invite – at

least twenty or even thirty.

D: Wow! Where do you know so many people around here from? You've not lived here that long, have you, Jill?

J: Well, some people make friends easily.

D: Wouldn't have thought you were one of those. Anyway, I have lots of people I want to invite, too.

A: OK, you win. So we've got something like sixty or seventy people – heaven knows where they'll all fit in, but that's your choice. Now. What about music?

D: Ah, well, I've already asked Martin to bring his stereo. You know he has this new stereo which is really great – and he has some really good party tapes.

J: Oh dear. We'd better warn the neighbours then, hadn't we?

A: Yes, I suppose so. Now, we'll also have to have two plans. One is a good weather plan, the other is a bad weather plan. If the weather's nice, we can have the food in the ...

D: Oh for heaven's sake, Andrew! Really! This isn't a military campaign. It's a party. Honestly, why don't you just let things be and see how they develop?

A: Listen, Don, this is not just dinner for three that we're planning. It's a party for seventy people. You've got to give them food, you've got to give them drink, and you have to have space for them. You can't improvise. Things must be planned – sorry.

J: Come on, you two, you're both overreacting. Why don't we all go into the kitchen and I'll make us some tea and we can calm down and discuss this rationally?

Now you'll hear Part 4 again.
(Part 4 repeated)
That's the end of Part 4. That's the end of the test.

Practice exam 3

Paper 1 – Reading

PART 1

1	G
2	F
3	A
4	C
5	B
6	E

PART 2

7	B
8	D
9	C
10	B
11	A
12	C
13	A

PART 3

14	A
15	D
16	E
17	G
18	B
19	F
20	H

PART 4

21	A
22	D
23	E
24	A
25	D
26	A
27	E
28	B

29	B
30	C
31	E
32	F
33	E
34	D
35	A

Paper 3 – Use of English

PART 1

1	B
2	C
3	A
4	D
5	B
6	D
7	B
8	D
9	B
10	C
11	A
12	A
13	A
14	D
15	C

PART 2

16	to
17	as
18	be
19	his
20	any
21	had
22	own/private/personal
23	than
24	on
25	down/downstairs
26	The/This/That
27	which/that
28	last/once
29	one/another
30	and

PART 3

31	wish you had learnt/learned to
32	as nice as working
33	as soon as Maria is
34	have not/haven't seen him since
35	give me a call/ring
36	about to leave the
37	have had enough of
38	is being dealt with by
39	makes no difference to
40	need to get is a

PART 4

41	the
42	to
43	✓
44	of
45	be
46	what
47	✓
48	✓
49	studying
50	at
51	the
52	to
53	✓
54	✓
55	more

PART 5

56	historic/historical
57	famous
58	collections
59	surprisingly
60	typical
61	lent
62	liking
63	sale
64	replacement
65	mysteriously

Paper 4 – Listening

PART 1

1	A
2	B
3	B
4	A
5	C
6	C
7	A
8	B

PART 2

9	catching criminals/solving crimes
10	identify criminals/keep files on criminals
11	identity card
12	the British/British officials
13	India
14	4/four types of fingerprints
15	catch criminals/a criminal
16	computer(s)
17	police experts
18	wear/are wearing gloves

PART 3

19	F
20	D
21	A
22	C
23	B

PART 4

24	D
25	B
26	B
27	M
28	B
29	B
30	D

Tapescript

Hello, I'm going to give you the instructions for this test. I'll introduce each part of the test and give you time to look at the questions. At the start of each piece you'll hear this sound. (tone) You'll hear each piece twice. Now look at Part 1.

PART 1

You'll hear people talking in eight different situations. For questions 1 to 8 choose the best answer, A, B or C.

Extract 1

A: Listen – you know the Sylvan Players?

B: Yes.

A: Well, we're giving a concert next Thursday and I thought you might like to come.

B: Oh – I didn't know you were involved with the group?

A: Oh, yes. I've been playing with them for years. I used to go to their concerts and then one of them asked me if I wanted to play with them.

B: Mmm. So how many times a week do you practise?

A: Oh, it varies. Before a concert we meet much more often because we need to bring things up to scratch. But otherwise it varies. Normally once a week, but sometimes less if people don't have time. You see, we don't want it to become boring or too much like work.

Extract 2

It was a great day in the lives of all supporters of the club when they got to the cup finals in 1975. You've got to remember that at that time, this place was very different from what it is now, and people identified with the local team. And what's more, we were always made fun of by the large, important teams. So to be there at the match, at the cup final with our boys, our own local team, was a great event.

Extract 3

A: So, what did you make of it?

B: I rather liked it. How about you?

A: Yes, I thought it was very good. But there's a problem with that hall – there are certain seats where you can't really hear very well. I mean, you know, when it was built, people said there were at least three rows in the middle where you couldn't hear. Well, I think we were sitting in one of those rows.

B: Well, I thought our seats were quite good. And we could see, which is important. You sometimes get seats at the back and you can't see half of what's happening on stage. And actually I understood every word.

Extract 4

Yes, my wife is extremely worried about it. You know, we have four children and in this heat it's very difficult without ... Yes, yes, I know you promised to come tomorrow, but it's been broken since last Friday. She did a large wash during the weekend, but the kids are going through a lot of clothes in this heat. My wife has to go out to work and she can't stand there and ... Right. So I'll expect you later this evening.

Extract 5

A: Good morning, Mrs Owen.

B: Good morning, John.

A: I'm sorry, but I have a lesson with Miss Smith tomorrow and I've had to make an emergency appointment with the dentist, so I won't be able to make the lesson. Do you think you could let her know? I don't have her phone number, but I'm sure you know how to get in touch with her. I don't want her to think I've forgotten the lesson or anything like that. I hope this isn't too much trouble.

B: No, that's OK. I'll write her a note telling her about it.

Extract 6

A: So how have the performances of *Persuasion* been going, Ruth?

B: Oh now I know why you look so familiar. I saw you act at the Edinburgh Festival.

C: Oh dear. How embarrassing.

B: No, I liked it. I remember you. You forgot your lines.

A: You didn't!

C: Yes, I did. I stood there in the middle of the stage thinking, 'Oh dear. What am I supposed to say now?' It was awful. But the audience was told that these were really previews. We knew we weren't ready – and they weren't actually paying .

B: Yes, yes, that's true – they warned us. Still, I must say that I really thought it was great, in spite of all the mistakes.

Extract 7

Hello, John. You asked me about that student. Well, she could take a language course, but that wouldn't really serve her needs. Then there's a preparatory course, which a lot of people are taking and which is accepted by universities as an entrance exam. ... Erm ... yes, I think that would be best. Of course she could also take one of the evening courses at the School of Extended Studies, but I doubt that would really give her what she wants either, so that really leaves you with the prepa— ... Yes, it is run by other universities ...

Extract 8

Experts as far away as New Zealand and the Soviet Union are keeping close tabs on Heartbeat Wales, the fitness campaign which aims to involve the whole Welsh population in a drive for better eating habits, less smoking and improved lifestyle. Surveys reveal that the message is getting across: forty percent of those questioned have changed to a healthier diet and twelve point five percent of smokers have given up. Restaurants compete for Heartbeat awards, which acknowledge the serving of nutritious dishes. And school dinners are being replaced with healthier alternatives.

That's the end of Part 1. Now look at Part 2.

PART 2

You'll hear a talk about the history of fingerprints. For questions 9 to 18, complete the notes which summarise what the speaker says. You will need to write a word or a short phrase in each box. You now have forty-five seconds in which to look at Part 2.

In a large number of countries in the late nineteenth century, an increasing number of experts were turning their minds towards the question of catching criminals. One very popular method was one I shall call 'The Measurement Method', simply because it relied on a number of measurements: the police would take measurements of a criminal's head, left foot, left middle finger, and left forearm, and put these measurements on file. You may well wonder how this method could help the police to solve crimes, since criminals very seldom are kind enough to leave their measurements on the scene of the crime. Well, it didn't. It did have one important use, though: at the time, it was very easy for criminals to give the police false names in order to avoid heavier sentences. Don't forget, this was before the time photography became widespread. What this method did was to help the police to keep files on criminals so they couldn't pretend to be someone else if they were caught committing another crime; so this was, in a way, like an identity

card. The system broke down, however, because of the notorious Fox twins from Hertfordshire. Because their measurements were almost identical, the police could never be sure which was which!

In South America, at the same time, the police were looking for a system for identifying criminals based on the measurement system. However, the South American experts were not really impressed with this system and its achievements, and they decided to experiment with fingerprinting. Fingerprints had already been previously used by British officials in India to prevent false pension claims. The South American experts developed a system of classifying fingerprints into four types, and, indeed, within a year this method proved itself and broke new ground when it was used to catch the first criminal using a fingerprint found on a door near the scene of the crime.

The system reached Britain in 1901 and immediately proved useful. And then, in 1930, Scotland Yard set up its first single fingerprint classification system to enable officers to compare fingerprints found on the scene of the crime with those of criminals known to the police. Fingerprint technology has advanced greatly since then. Different types of powder are used to strengthen the impression of the fingerprint before it is taken. For example, on hard, shiny surfaces, aluminium powder is used. Laser technology is also used. Another revolution has been in the way that fingerprints are identified. Not long ago, a fingerprint would first be brought to the Scotland Yard expert, who would look at it and then start searching among the thousands of fingerprints which might match it. Today, the first search is done by computer, which then produces a selection of possible matches. The final identification, however, is done by police experts.

Finally, it is important to explode one myth: using gloves will not prevent a fingerprint from being taken.

Now you'll hear Part 2 again.
(Part 2 repeated)
That's the end of Part 2. Now look at Part 3.

PART 3

You'll hear five different people talking about holidays they had. For questions 19 to 23, choose from the list A to F which kind of holiday each person had. Use the letters only once. There is one extra letter which you do not need to use. You now have thirty seconds to look through Part 3.

Speaker 1

Oh, it was absolutely wonderful! We started at Maidenhead and then we spent a whole week going through the most gorgeous countryside. There are some wonderful villages on the way, on both sides. Every night we'd sleep somewhere else. We'd get off and put up a tent in a field. It took us about four days, really, from Maidenhead to Lechlade and then three days back from Lechlade to Maidenhead because of the currents. You know, it takes longer when you're sailing upstream, against the current. And ... oh ... we went through some really wonderful unspoilt scenery on the way – very, very beautiful, very calm, very relaxing. It was one of the most wonderful holidays I've ever had.

Speaker 2

Well, the area is still relatively unspoilt, with beautiful mountains. What we did was, we left our car at one spot, at a youth hostel, and we walked from one youth hostel to the next, walking around the country from one place to another. There was always another youth hostel within walking distance. Although the area is on the whole mountainous, we didn't really actually have to climb any mountains because the routes are quite ... well, let's put it this way – you don't have to climb mountains if you don't want to and because I'm not really good at that, we didn't. So even for someone my age it was quite easy.

Speaker 3

Oh, I loved it. I really love the feeling of not having to do anything, just get up in the morning, go for a quick swim, then come back and have breakfast at the hotel, maybe go for a short walk, come back and lie in the sun a bit till lunch. And the wonderful thing is that there's no pollution. You don't get these horrible creatures in the water that you get in other places and you don't come back from your morning swim feeling all oily and greasy because the water's polluted. Wonderful place. Definitely recommended.

Speaker 4

You know, the scenery was really rewarding. I mean, I've been doing this for years now, and mostly it has been the physical achievement. I would train incredibly hard; places did not exist for themselves, they existed for the challenge, the battle with nature, and the technical expertise of handling the ropes and the equipment. It was really centred on myself – I am doing this. But this time it was different. I would get to the top and I would look down all round and think, 'Wow, what a marvellous view!'

Speaker 5

I was a bit worried at the beginning. It's true that I'd been keeping fit and jogging so that I would be able to do it. Most of the people in our group were much younger than me and I thought I wouldn't be able to keep up with them. They would all be overtaking me and speeding way ahead. I had these terrible visions of having a flat tyre and having to repair it, of being left behind by everyone else, all alone. But in the end it turned out that we were all more or less at the same level and we really had a great time.

Now you'll hear Part 3 again.
(Part 3 repeated)
That's the end of Part 3. Now look at Part 4.

PART 4

You'll hear a conversation between three people who are going for a meal together. Answer questions 24 to 30 by writing B (for Bridget), M (for Maria) or D (for Daniel). You now have thirty seconds to look through Part 4.

B = Bridget   M = Maria   D = Daniel

B: Right, well, I'm glad that we're finally managing to go somewhere together, the three of us. It's been ages, hasn't it? Anyway, I suppose the first thing to decide is whether we want to have dinner before we go to the theatre or after the play. What do you say, Maria?

M: I don't really mind. Either will do.

D: I don't know. I'm going to have to stay at work quite late today, I think, and I'm not sure I'm going to be able to make it if we decide to eat before the play.

M: Yes, I agree with Daniel, we should eat after the play. So where should we go ...

D: On the other hand, if we go for dinner after the play that means we'll get home very late and I

B: have to be at work early tomorrow, so maybe ...

B: Oh, come on, Daniel. Enough's enough. Decide. You can't have it both ways. Either before or after.

D: Calm down, Bridget! I'm sorry, but I don't think that ...

B: Right, OK. After it is. Now, where are we going?

D: Well, Bridget, I was thinking of that French place on the high street? What's it called, Maria? You know the one I mean? It's recently changed hands. It used to have a different name.

M: Oh, yes. 'Michel's' – it's a great place. I love it. Excellent food. Really good. Probably the best food in town.

B: Erm, do they have a good vegetarian selection? Cause very often in that sort of place you can't really get a proper meal if you don't eat meat.

D: Why? Surely you're not a vegetarian, Bridget?

B: Oh, yes I am. I stopped eating meat a year ago. Haven't you noticed? That's not very observant of you.

D: Well, it's a very long time since you last did me the honour of having dinner with me. You're busier than the Prime Minister!

B: So. What about 'Michel's'? Will they have a vegetarian selection?

M: Mmm. Maybe not. Their big thing is steak. What about the new restaurant next to it? It's also supposed to be very good.

D: No way. I looked in once and it's terribly smoky and stuffy.

M: Oh, come on, you two. We've got to decide. Bridget, what about 'Michel's' then? I'm sure they'll come up with something?

B: Oh, well. Alright.

Now you'll hear Part 4 again.
(Part 4 repeated)
That's the end of Part 4. That's the end of the test.

Practice exam 4

Paper 1 – Reading

PART 1

1	B
2	H
3	G
4	E
5	C
6	D
7	F

PART 2

8	C
9	B
10	D
11	C
12	B
13	A
14	A

PART 3

15	B
16	D
17	F
18	H
19	C
20	A
21	E

PART 4

22	A
23	C
24	E
25	D
26	G
27	A
28	D

29	E
30	B
31	D
32	A
33	F
34	C
35	E

Paper 3 – Use of English

PART 1

1	A
2	B
3	A
4	D
5	C
6	C
7	A
8	A
9	C
10	B
11	A
12	D
13	A
14	C
15	B

PART 2

16	where
17	another
18	rather
19	long
20	fewer
21	of
22	was
23	had
24	under/beneath
25	how
26	One
27	be
28	Whatever
29	never
30	what

PART 3

31   is said to be the
32   to avoid getting caught
33   should have been told
34   more beautifully than anybody/anyone
35   miss my train unless I
36   about going for
37   seems to have developed amazingly
38   had not/hadn't reminded me
39   am not used to going
40   how thankful I

PART 4

41   has
42   was
43   than
44   a
45   ✓
46   ✓
47   be
48   of
49   the
50   of
51   to
52   ✓
53   ✓
54   more
55   ✓

PART 5

56   threatened
57   polluted
58   disappearance
59   scientists
60   defence/defense
61   completely
62   driving
63   household
64   decision
65   ensure

Paper 4 – Listening

PART 1

1   C
2   C
3   B
4   A
5   A
6   B
7   C
8   A

PART 2

9   three rooms/two bedrooms
10   north of the station
11   10/ten minutes on foot/a ten-minute walk
12   unfurnished
13   £550/five hundred and fifty pounds
     a/per month
14   April 1st/first of April
15   (at least) one year
16   on the ground floor
17   near a playground
18   near a school
(17 and 18 in any order)

PART 3

19   C
20   D
21   E
22   B
23   A

PART 4

24   C
25   C
26   A
27   B
28   B
29   C
30   B

Tapescript

Hello. I'm going to give you the instructions for this test. I'll introduce each part of the test and give you time to look at the questions. At the start of each piece you'll hear this sound. (tone) You'll hear each piece twice. Now look at Part 1.

PART 1

You'll hear people talking in eight different situations. For questions 1 to 8, choose the best answer, A, B or C.

Extract 1

A: Hello, madam. Are you ready to order?

B: Hi. Yes. Listen, I have to leave within forty minutes. Do I have enough time to have today's special menu?

A: Yes, madam, no problem. It won't take long.

B: Right, now, if I take the full special lunch menu, can I change the vegetables? I'd like to have the chicken, but I'd like to have boiled potatoes instead of chips, and I want to have a green salad instead of beans.

A: No, madam, I'm afraid I can't do that.

B: In that case can I order just two side dishes?

A: No, sorry again. You've got to order a main dish during lunch time.

B: Oh, alright. I'll have the full meal then. That's really a pity. Are you sure you really can't ... ?

Extract 2

A: Excuse me, can anyone use the rooms in this building?

B: Well, it depends. Are you a student in the music department?

A: Well, I am taking private lessons with one of the piano teachers here, but I'm not a registered student in the department, not really.

B: Right, well, the rules are that if you're a student in the music department, you can use the building at any time. You get a key and you can enter when you like. Other people can use the building between nine and five, but they are not allowed to reserve a room; they can only use the practice rooms if they are free.

Extract 3

A: Mmm. They look very nice. Do you grill them one by one?

B: Yes, it's better that way.

A: Now, why's that?

B: Well, they grill very quickly, as you can all see ... and the moment they're ready you've got to take them off because they burn immediately – ah, ah – there we go. Let's just hold it up. You see, this is the colour you should be aiming for – any darker than this and it starts tasting burnt. There. Now let's put another one on.

A: Mmm. This is very good. Really nice and crispy. You can also fry them, can't you?

B: Yes, but you need to deep-fry them, and it takes a lot of oil, so I recommend grilling. It's also much healthier, of course.

Extract 4

Hi, Janet. Listen, I'm calling to find out if you're free tonight because we've got tickets for the theatre. We had everything fixed – Maureen was going to babysit for us, but in the end it turns out there was a mix up in the dates and she can't make it. ... Oh, yes, that's very kind of you. ... Yes. We've talked about it and what we've decided to do is that John will stay with the children while we ... So how about it? It's had very good reviews. I know this is a bit late, but I thought it would be the best thing to do. ... Oh, alright, don't worry, I'll find someone else.

Extract 5

On one occasion I was sixth on the standby list for a flight from – well, I think I'd better not mention the country. Unfortunately, there were only three seats left, but the check-in staff asked if we'd like to sit on each others' laps for take-off and landing. Well, we all agreed, as that was the only way of getting there. At the last moment the captain decided he'd rather not lose his licence. The flight did get there, but unfortunately we were not on board.

Extract 6

When people started earning more, they wanted larger houses, but the plots were very small, so they re-built the houses and some people built a second storey. Those who had big money rebuilt their house totally. Other people took down a lot of internal walls and totally restructured the house. We could only afford to break down one external wall and build a small extension. But the thing is that the neighbourhood is now considered so desirable that even a house like this, which we've done very little to, can fetch a very high price.

Extract 7

A: Hello. How may I help?

B: Good afternoon. I got this note requesting that I return this book and I was wondering why – I still have some time on it.

A: Well, that is probably because someone else has requested it. Can I have your library card?

B: Yes.

A: Erm ... ah, yes, I see. It seems that the book was issued to you by mistake, because you already had ten books out and this was the eleventh. Really the system should not have allowed you to take this book out, so I'm afraid you have to return it.

B: Can't I hold on to it for a week longer?

A: No, sir. I'm afraid we really must insist.

Extract 8

Well, what happens is that when he comes back from his holiday, he finds that someone has got into his flat and cleaned it out completely. They must have had a key somehow because there is no sign of a break-in. They got special permission from the police to park their van outside the house while they were unloading – the oldest trick in the book. And it's quite funny because you see him standing there, the room is totally empty and all you see is his legs and the computer in the middle of the room. Oh, quite an effective shot I must say. The script was written by the man who wrote ...

That's the end of Part 1. Now look at Part 2.

PART 2

You'll hear a man who is looking for a flat talking to an estate agent about the type of flat that he wants to rent. For questions 9 to18, fill in the estate agent's form. You will need to write a word or a short phrase in each box. You now have forty-five seconds in which to look at Part 2.

E = estate agent   C = customer

E: Good morning. Can I help you?

C: Hi. I'm looking for an apartment to rent and I wanted to talk to you about what you had to offer right now.

E: Yes, of course. Let me first take down a few details about what you're looking for to see whether there's anything I can offer you, and then I'll take a few personal details if that's OK. So. First of all the size of the flat – what kind of flat are you looking for? How large?

C: Well, I'm not sure because I don't know what I can afford, but ideally I suppose I would look for three rooms – so it's what you would call a two-bedroom flat here.

E: Right – so two bedrooms. And have you thought where?

C: Well, I need to take the train to work and in the evenings I often stay at work and come home quite late, so I guess the general area would be north of the station.

E: Fine, yes, this seems logical, although of course flats near the station are quite expensive. How far away from the station are you willing to consider?

C: Well, I suppose if it's basically about a fifteen-minute walk away from the station, that's OK – no, actually, let's say ten minutes from the station. Yes, ten minutes is the farthest I would be willing to go.

E: OK. And how much are you willing to pay?

C: How much do you think somewhere like this will cost me?

E: Well, it depends of course on other things, though mainly on whether it's furnished, unfurnished or partly furnished. Have you thought of that?

C: Yes, and we're going for an unfurnished flat.

E: Well, in that case you're slightly better off, but still in this area the least you'd expect to pay is probably £400 a month – and that won't get you a nice place. If you want something nice, you'll have to be willing to pay more.

C: Right. Well, let's say up to £550, no more.

E: Good. Now, about time – when do you need to move in?

C: I definitely need a place for April 1st. And I would want to have a contract for at least a year.

E: OK. Any other points you would want to make before we start looking?

C: Yes. Firstly, it's got to be on the ground floor; and then we've got two young kids, so preferably I'd like the flat to be near a children's playground, and then a school. But these two requirements – near the playground, and near a school – these two are not that important because we can always manage with the car.

E: OK. Now if you would just give me a few personal details – your name ...

Now you'll hear Part 2 again.
(Part 2 repeated)
That's the end of Part 2. Now look at Part 3.

PART 3

You'll hear five different women talking about their jobs. For questions 19 to 23, choose from the list A to F which kind of job each person does. Use the letters only once. There is one extra letter which you do not need to use. You now have thirty seconds to look through Part 3.

Speaker 1

A lot of people complain about this place, but I love it. The main problem is that you're required to work almost every evening, so you don't have free time, but that's when the place is really busy. Some of my friends feel that it's not very good to be on your feet for so long, but I enjoy running from table to table. In fact, the more tables I have, the better it is. It gets really hectic and stressful and I love it!

Speaker 2

Well, it's not the greatest job in the world. Basically it's clerical work. It entails a lot of cataloguing and going round the shelves and putting everything back. You'd be surprised how many students have no idea where to put the books. Oh, I enjoyed it much more when I worked in a smaller place and I had contact with people. I knew a lot about the topics they were reading about and I felt that I could help them find what they were looking for.

Speaker 3

Well, it's good if you like serving people and if you enjoy solving small problems quickly, because people will come up to you, ask a question or two, expect quick answers and then go. You've got to be quite efficient, but you can't hurry things. If you need the computer to print a bill, it will do so at its own pace and you can't do a thing. So if a guest is in a hurry, it's up to you to keep them happy. Or if a large group arrives exactly when another large group is checking out – that can be quite difficult.

Speaker 4

I find it quite boring. I mean, there's not a lot of variety in what you do. I came to work here because I thought I would advance fairly quickly, but up till now it's been quite boring. You've got to be accurate and you can't make mistakes, but basically all the operations are the same, really. Most clients at our branch have the same type of account and are carrying out the same financial transactions, so people come up to you with exactly the same types of problem.

Speaker 5

It suits me. It's not the most interesting work in the world, but it's a nice combination of working with people and working with the boss, doing what other people ask you to do and deciding on your own agenda. Margaret, who worked here before me, she couldn't get used to using the computer. She was perfectly happy typing letters or memos on the typewriter, which she preferred. I think that in the last few years when she was having to use the computer to do all the administrative stuff for the department, she wasn't very happy – and it showed.

Now you'll hear Part 3 again.
(Part 3 repeated)
That's the end of Part 3. Now look at Part 4

PART 4

You'll hear part of a radio programme about a sports event. For questions 24 to 30, decide which of the choices, A, B or C is the correct answer. You now have one minute to look through Part 4.

A = announcer   SJ = Stewart Johnson

A: One of the most exciting events this summer is the Richmond Festival of Sport, taking place in Richmond between May 27th and June 4th. Here to tell us about it is Stewart Johnson.

SJ: Well, this is an especially exciting time for us because of the large number of new events we're offering this year. We're in our ninth year now, and we're on our way to becoming one of the largest events of our kind in the country. And probably the secret of our success is that we offer what is, really, a unique mixture of participation and spectator events, which means that everybody can take part in one way or another, either being active in the sport of their choice or cheering their favourite team.

Now on the whole, the festival is intended for all ages, but Fun Sessions are special. Although anyone can take part, we've structured them so that they're in fact aimed at children and intended for them to try out new skills and practise them – and at the same time have fun. Equipment is provided, and we have qualified instructors at hand at every session. So all you have to do is bring your kids along! Amongst the sports we are offering this year are golf, squash, karate, fencing, and, for the first time this year, tennis as well. I think most of us realise how important it is to start practising sports from a young age, so don't miss this opportunity to get your child involved. This is a gift for life!

From May 30th to June 2nd we will be holding a Watersports Activity Course at the Royal Canoe Club, and participants will have the chance to try various sports such as rowing, sailing and canoeing, and the event will end with a fun regatta to give young people the chance to put their newly learnt skills to the test. Children will be split into age groups for the activities and must be capable of swimming a hundred metres in light clothing. Unlike most events taking place this week numbers on these courses have to be limited, because we need to make sure that we have enough boats and canoes and so on, and unfortunately we've got to insist that parents register their children at least a week before the event, erm, simply because this gives us time to organise the necessary equipment, and we're asking for a registration fee of £5 to make sure that people turn up.

Erm, another important part of the whole event is the competitions that we hold. These competitions will be going on throughout the week, and Sunday 4th June promises to be an especially exciting day with the final match in each sport taking place. Well, I said earlier that our activities are intended for all ages, and I'd like to end with a mention of the Fun Run, which signals the end of the festival, erm, and if you enjoy running but don't enjoy competing, this is the event for you. People of all ages – families, children, senior citizens – everybody is invited to take part, and in fact our oldest participant up till now has been an 82-year-old woman – the oldest participant, in fact, in an amateur event in Britain. And if she comes back this year she will help us beat our own record – and hers – and become at 83 the oldest participant in an amateur event. Or maybe one of our listeners would like to try and beat that? We'll be happy if you do!

Now you'll hear Part 4 again.
(Part 4 repeated)
That's the end of Part 4. That's the end of the test.

Practice exam 5

Paper 1 – Reading

PART 1

1	D
2	G
3	H
4	A
5	B
6	E
7	C

PART 2

8	D
9	B
10	A
11	D
12	B
13	C
14	A

PART 3

15	G
16	F
17	H
18	B
19	C
20	E
21	D

PART 4

22	A
23	C
24	A
25	B
26	D
27	E
28	C

29	D
30	D
31	E
32	B
33	A
34	B
35	D

Paper 3 – Use of English

PART 1

1	D
2	B
3	A
4	C
5	B
6	C
7	C
8	A
9	B
10	C
11	A
12	D
13	A
14	D
15	C

PART 2

16	However
17	cases/instances
18	its
19	were
20	well
21	and/while/as
22	that
23	from
24	which/that
25	more/some/greater/increased
26	their
27	each
28	one
29	had
30	on

PART 3

31 new school should be built
32 was brought up very traditionally/
    was very traditionally brought up
33 hardly (ever) go out these
34 was always being told what
35 she did not/didn't look happy
36 she could lend him
37 is out of the question
38 was too short to visit
39 my warning they climbed that
40 one of the few people

PART 4

41 ✓
42 ✓
43 very
44 it
45 us
46 ✓
47 to
48 being
49 the
50 ✓
51 she
52 to
53 ✓
54 me
55 them

PART 5

56 impossible
57 storage
58 fishermen
59 unaware
60 existence
61 unable
62 length
63 technological
64 coastal
65 discoveries

Paper 4 – Listening

PART 1

1 C
2 C
3 B
4 B
5 C
6 B
7 A
8 B

PART 2

9   five years ago
10 (greater) reductions (on tickets)
11 a regular commercial cinema
12 three months ago
13 The Third Man
14 once a month
15 foreign language films
16 leaflets
17 (the) club
18 (the) University

PART 3

19 C
20 A
21 E
22 F
23 B

PART 4

24 T
25 F
26 T
27 T
28 F
29 F
30 F

Tapescript

Hello. I'm going to give you the instructions for this test. I'll introduce each part of the test and give you time to look at the questions. At the start of each piece you'll hear this sound. (tone) You'll hear each piece twice. Now look at Part 1.

PART 1

You'll hear people talking in eight different situations. For questions 1 to 8, choose the best answer, A, B or C.

Extract 1

A: So how long have you been living here?
B: Mmm ... well, I came last September.
A: And where are you living at the moment?
B: I'm staying in a University Hall near Gordon Square – it's only for students coming from the Commonwealth. It's the best location in town, and it's amazingly cheap. You get a very good social life and meet a lot of people.
A: And what exactly are you doing? You said earlier you were a lawyer?
B: Well, not exactly. I'm training actually ...

Extract 2

A: It's making a terrible noise. I hate those alarms that go off like that. I wonder how long it's going to take them to get here.
B: Well, the guard has to drive to the administration building, get a key, drive back here – it can take up to ten or fifteen minutes.
A: That's not good enough, is it? By that time someone could have stolen half the equipment. I wonder what happened to set it off. Can't you turn it off?
B: No. You need to be able to get into this control board which tells you which room it's been set off in, and they come here and check that everything's alright.
A: Well, we don't even know which room it's in, do we?

Extract 3

Hello, this is John here. I got your message about missing me at lunchtime today and I realised that it was Mike's farewell party. I simply went to lunch and the party totally slipped out of my mind. It's just that I got the note so long ago. I do hope he won't think that I didn't feel like going. Can you tell him that I was really looking forward to seeing him and I

wish him all the best in the future? Thanks. Bye.

Extract 4

A: Hello. Mary Carter speaking.
B: Hello, Mary, John here. About the meeting tomorrow ...
A: Yes, about the new offices?
B: Yes. Is it alright if we have the meeting at your office instead of mine? It's simply that I'm going to be near your office for another meeting and it would be easier for me if we did it that way.
A: Oh, well, the problem is that I've asked Martin to come along and he will be coming straight to your office after inspecting the new building.
B: Can't you let him know about the change?
A: No – he's away and there's no way I can get in touch with him before tomorrow.
B: Ah, well, so we'll have to leave it as it is.

Extract 5

If the unpredictable British weather prevents you from getting to the seaside this summer, the themes of sun, sea and sand are being celebrated indoors in a number of galleries around the country. 'Beside the seaside' in York has gathered the work of UK artists whose work focuses on images of that strange world where land and sea meet. All exhibits shown can be bought by visitors, including ceramic life-size ducks. In Scarborough you can see the award-winning exhibition 'Holiday in a lunch hour', where lunchtime visitors to the gallery are guaranteed sunshine by being taken to holiday locations of their choice through computer technology. And no money is wasted on sun-cream.

Extract 6

A: Excuse me, I'm not sure that I've got this right. Is the next train into town leaving at 10:45 from Platform 5?
B: Yes, that's correct. But there's one slightly later which is a fast train and will get you there earlier. It leaves from Platform 8.
A: Yes, but I'm not sure that my ticket is valid for that. I haven't paid – what do you call it? – the supplement for the fast train.
B: Oh, you don't need to pay a supplement for a fast train. Any ticket for your destination is valid.
A: Ah, good, so I can take that one?
B: Yes, and it leaves from Platform 8.
A: Thanks.

Extract 7

You know that cookbook for dieting that you mentioned – *Diet with Taste*? Well, it really looks great ... Yes, well, I'm not sure about the photographs, they're a bit too ... Yes, well, I'm not convinced that it really does help people lose weight. It claims you can eat as much as you like as long as you stick to the foods they recommend and I've had bad experiences with that sort of thing. Oh, but she has recipes from all over the world, so you never get bored. Anyway I thought I'd get it even if it won't necessarily help me to lose weight.

Extract 8

Well, I use my bike to get to work. It still is the best way of getting about, but I find it quite hazardous – you really have to be extremely careful. There's the pollution problem, for one, because you're breathing in all the fumes from the cars, but in addition there are all sorts of other dangers. Basically, cars and lorries don't recognise our presence and they tend to squeeze us off the road. They drive extremely close to you, they take a turn right in front of you and they don't even use their indicator! And there are drivers who chuck burning cigarettes out of their windows, and you have holes in the streets, and then there's all the broken glass on the roads which causes so many punctures ...

That's the end of Part 1. Now look at Part 2.

PART 2

You'll hear a woman being interviewed about her film-watching habits. For questions 9 to 18, complete the questionnaire which the interviewer fills in. You will need to write a word or a short phrase in each box. You now have forty-five seconds in which to look at Part 2.

A: Good evening. I'm from the staff here at the Progress Film Club. We're having a survey of our clients, and I wondered if you would be willing to help by answering a few questions while you're waiting to go in to see the film?

B: Yes, of course.

A: Well, the first question is: are you or have you ever been a member of the Progress Film Club?

B: Well, yes, I used to be a member for a number of years, but then there was a period when I left town – that was five years ago. When I came back, I never bothered to join again, so I haven't been a member for the past five years.

A: What things would make you want to become a member?

B: Well, as far as I know members don't really have a say in choosing the films that are brought here, that's one thing to consider, but I think maybe the main thing is that there are very few advantages in actually being a member. For example, you don't really get such a large reduction on the cost of a ticket if you're a member.

A: So – greater reductions?

B: Yes.

A: OK ... next question: where do you prefer to see films?

B: Well, this is a slightly embarrassing question to answer here at the club. I mean, I do like seeing films here, and I also like seeing films on TV or video, but really, where I'd rather see films is in a regular commercial cinema.

A: That's alright – no need to be embarrassed. When did you last see a film at the Progress Film Club?

B: Oh, I can't remember. I think the last film I saw here was *The Third Man*. When was that? ... About six weeks ago, I think.

A: Well, *The Third Man* was actually shown three months ago.

B: Oh, really? Well, must have been then.

A: Right. You've actually answered my next question which is: what was the last film you saw here? ... so ... *The Third Man*. You don't go to see films at the Progress Film Club very often then, do you?

B: It depends, really. There are times when I go once a week, if there are a lot of films that interest me. Other times, as you've heard, I don't go for months on end.

A: Well, I've got to put only one figure in here, so what would you say, on average?

B: Erm ... once a month.

A: OK. OK. Which type of film do you think we should show more of at the club?

B: Foreign language films. I think that there is a real lack of films from other countries and in other languages here.

A: OK. Now, we have had a very strong publicity drive in the past few months, and I'm sure you've noticed that.

B: Yes, I have.

A: Which type of advert have you seen most?

B: Well, mostly the leaflets.

A: And where did you see them?

B: Well, in two places. Firstly, here, at the club, and secondly at the University. There are lots of them around there.

A: Right, OK. That's it. Thanks a lot.

B: Oh, that's alright. I enjoyed this – gave me

something to do while queuing.

Now you'll hear Part 2 again.
(Part 2 repeated)
That's the end of Part 2. Now look at Part 3.

PART 3

You'll hear five different men talk about why they are learning a new language. For questions 19 to 23, choose from the list A to F which reason each person mentions. Use the letters only once. There is one extra letter which you do not need to use. You now have thirty seconds to look through Part 3.

Speaker 1

Well, you see I came here last year to teach English, and it was the first time I'd ever gone to work in a country whose language I didn't know. After a while I realised that in order to get along I would need to know the language because although some people speak English, this doesn't get you very far. Even at work not everybody understands instructions that I give in English – when I want photocopying done and so on – and it just helps contact with people generally.

Speaker 2

Well, at school I did Latin and Greek, and later you had the option of doing a modern language. I did French, which really set the scene. Then at university I read Modern Languages and now I have a degree in French and German. And for my birthday my wife gave me a book called *Italian is easy if you know Latin* and I thought to myself, 'Hmm, let's see how fast I can learn Italian.' In fact, it took me only a few weeks till I was able not only to read but also to speak and listen to the radio, and even write fairly well.

Speaker 3

Well, my wife is a lecturer in the German Department and at home she is always going on about how the greatest writers of the twentieth century are German, so I read the translations. But then she started saying how these translations do not really capture the spirit of the original and how I should really learn German in order to be able to appreciate these novels. And, frankly, she does have a point there and so in the end I decided that I would learn German.

Speaker 4

I don't really like learning foreign languages. I find them incredibly difficult. But I suppose one has to learn them, simply because everywhere you look now you find advertisements looking for secretaries with at least one foreign language. And obviously you stand a better chance anywhere if you have an additional language. So I decided to take up French again. I did it at school, but was never really any good at it. But I thought maybe this time it would be easier – which unfortunately it isn't.

Speaker 5

Well, my girlfriend is living in South America and she of course is a Spanish speaker. I am going out there to visit her, so I thought that I should really have a few words of the language to be able to get along. I mean, I suppose I could get by with English, but I would like to be on the safe side, and, although I'll be back within a couple of weeks, it will still be fun to have tried to learn a bit of the language and to have tried to use it. I mean, we always assume that other people will know English. It's a mark of respect if we try to learn their language, too.

Now you'll hear Part 3 again.
(Part 3 repeated)
That's the end of Part 3. Now look at Part 4.

PART 4

You'll hear a talk about a new bridge that is going to be built. For questions 24 to 30, decide whether the statement in the question is True or False. If it is True, write T on your answer sheet. If it is False, write F on your answer sheet. You now have thirty seconds to look through Part 4.

A = announcer   HE = Helen Edridge

A: Next week one of the most important local issues will be put to the vote in the local council: whether to build a new bridge over the river or not. The question will be settled once and for all. With us today is Dr Helen Edridge to talk about her view of the matter.

HE: Well, there's been quite a controversy raging about building an additional bridge over the river and this controversy has been going on for many years now, but I must say that this has become a full-scale war ever since concrete suggestions were made to build the bridge. It's been a very long campaign, with a lot of accusations flying about – accusations of being narrow-minded, short-sighted, even accusations of corruption, which were later proven to be invented – in short, not a pretty campaign. I think that for me the main question is whether this bridge will, indeed, free the town centre from traffic, and I think I can safely say that almost everyone agrees that for some time it will do that. The logic is really quite simple. Instead of crossing the river on one of the two existing bridges, both of which are in the centre of town, drivers will cross the river before they even come into town. The centre will be quieter, more people will come into the centre and we will all finally be able to enjoy the town again. But – and this is a big 'but' – this will happen for only a very short period. The long-term effect may, in fact, be utterly and totally different. The sad truth is that roads attract traffic, and because there will now be an easy way to cross the river, more people will do so. The committee reporting on building the bridge recognised this when saying that the increasing number of vehicles would come because – and I quote – 'the new bridge would provide a shortcut between the industrial north and the ports in the south, and will make this route particularly attractive to traffic connecting the two areas. This will result in great economic benefits to the area.'

The result will be that the new bridge will be packed. More cars, especially more lorries, will be passing through the area. Pollution will undoubtedly rise. In fact, the prediction is that twice as many cars will take the north-south route than are currently taking the present one, which, compared to the situation five years ago, is an increase of at least ten times. And then, because roads attract traffic, as I said earlier, the route will become so packed that drivers will once more go back to driving through the town centre and crossing the river there. So, after being attractive for a short period, the centre will once again be full of cars and empty of people, which may badly affect the economic development of the area. So, really, I think that what will happen ...

Now you'll hear Part 4 again.
(Part 4 repeated)
That's the end of Part 4. That's the end of the test.